Balnagown

Balnagown

ancestral home of the Clan Ross

Balnagown

ancestral home of the Clan Ross

A Scottish Castle Through Five Centuries

with photography by Fritz von der Schulenburg

Main photography by Fritz von der Schulenburg

First published in 1997 by

BROMPTON PRESS

100, Brompton Road, London SW3 1ER

British Library Cataloguing in Publication Data
A catalogue record for this book is available from
the British Library

ISBN 1 900055 07 4

Design: Conway Smith Design
Production: Deer Park Productions

Picture origination by Corinium Digital Imaging, Swindon
Printed and bound by Arnoldo Mondadori Editore, Verona, Italy

ENDPAPERS: Wallpaper in the Dining Room of Balnagown, copy of mid-
nineteenth century original.
HALF TITLE: The castle from the south-west, an Edwardian postcard.
FRONTISPIECE: The west front in 1958.
TITLE PAGE: Seal of the Earl of Ross, thirteenth century.
OPPOSITE: Bust of Sir Charles Ross, the last of the Lockhart Ross lairds,
by Moses Dykaar.

The publishers would like to thank the following for their assistance:
Tam Coyle (Factor of the Balnagown Estates), Elaine Smith (formerly of the
Balnagown Estates), Tim Dale, Estelle Quick (Curator of the Tain & District
Museum), Simon Green of the National Monuments Record of Scotland, and
the staff of the National Galleries of Scotland, the National Library of Scotland
(Map Library) and the Scottish Record Office.

The History

A Tour of the Castle

The warlike dead of every age

Who fill the fair recording page

   Shall leave their sainted rest,

And half-reclining on his spear

Each wondering chief by turns appear

   To hail the blooming guest.

WILLIAM COLLINS
'Ode on the Death of Colonel Charles Ross', 1745.

Balnagown

ancestral home of the Clan Ross

A MILE OR SO INLAND from Nigg Bay, on a hill above the fertile coastland of Easter Ross, stands Balnagown Castle. Its pink-harled walls and reddish sandstone masonry contrast brightly with the greenery and the woodland along the Balnagown River. For centuries this was the home of the Chiefs of the Clan Ross, once the most powerful of the Highland

clans. Many of the castles that were built around here in the middle ages are now ruins or have vanished. Balnagown is one of the few to have remained continuously inhabited since it was erected, probably in the fifteenth century. Throughout those five hundred years the Ross lairds of Balnagown played their part in the history of the kingdom, as leaders of their clan, soldiers and politicians, agricultural reformers, brigands and benefactors. In the words of the novelist and historian Nigel Tranter, 'the Rosses were a lively lot'.

The castle has grown over the centuries, adapted by its owners to changing times. The medieval core, a simple tower-house, gradually extended and transformed, had by the end of the nineteenth century become a comfortable gentleman's country seat. The present owner,

LEFT: *The castle rising majestically above Balnagown Wood, with the hills of the Black Isle beyond.*
ABOVE: *A turret of the east wing, built in the nineteenth century in medieval style.*

Mohamed Al Fayed, who rescued the dilapidated property from ruin in 1972 to make it his Scottish home, has recently undertaken a thorough restoration and conservation programme, preserving the fabric for future generations. Over the last twenty-five years he has also revitalized the running of Balnagown's estates, comprising large tracts of agricultural and sporting land, which had formerly faced bankruptcy.

The Land of Ross

BALNAGOWN OWED ITS IMPORTANCE to the vicissitudes of history and to its geographical location. The castle stands on the southern side of an anvil-shaped promontory extending into the Moray Firth. To the north is the Dornoch Firth, while to the south the Cromarty Firth separates this peninsula from the Black Isle.

Visitors not familiar with this part of Scotland often expect a bleak and wild landscape, so it is a surprise to find that the climate is generally mild and that the low-lying arable land of this coastal region is some of the most fertile in the British Isles. There are other advantages too. The inlets in the coastline, especially the deep water harbour of the Cromarty Firth, provided safe anchorage long before the Royal Navy made its base at Invergordon. Over the centuries the sea has brought danger – the devastation wrought by the Viking raids of the eighth and ninth centuries, for example – but it has also been a vital means of communication, especially in the centuries before the construction of modern roads in the Highlands.

Facing north to Sutherland across the Dornoch Firth is the small but ancient burgh of Tain. The relics of the eleventh-century Saint Duthac became one of Scotland's most important centres of pilgrimage in the later middle ages. King James IV was one of the thousands of pilgrims who made their way to Tain along the road that leads past Balnagown. For centuries the Lairds of Balnagown played a prominent role in the municipal life of Tain, serving as Provosts and Members of Parliament.

Inland, away from the peninsula, the straths and glens lead away into harsher, less hospitable terrain: the Highlands. The Great Glen, the rift valley bisecting the Highland region south-west of Inverness, has always been an important route linking the east and west coasts. Today the sparsely populated Highland region of Scotland is one of the last wild areas of Europe, but for much of Balnagown's history a hardy people eked out an increasingly precarious existence farming here, before the region was brutally depopulated in the

TOP: *The weathered tomb of Findlay McFaed, a fifteenth-century abbot, still survives in the roofless south aisle of Fearn Abbey church.*
ABOVE: *The River Cassley with the Highlands in the distance.*
OPPOSITE: *The Balnagown River flows past the foot of the castle.*

eighteenth and nineteenth centuries.

Although Balnagown Castle itself is near the coast, its lands extended west and north across the Highlands. Here lived many of the Ross clansmen, bound to their Chief by an ancestral loyalty.

The early centuries saw a variety of cultural influences in this part of Scotland. Until the ninth century AD it was part of the northern Pictish kingdom. The Picts, or 'painted people' (so called by the Romans because of their tattoos), seem to have been a Celtic confederation of tribes. Some of these were identified in the second century AD by the geographer Ptolemy of Alexandria: the inhabitants of Easter Ross were the *Decantæ*, while the *Lugi*, *Smertæ* and *Cornavii* lived further north in Sutherland and Caithness. On the west coast different tribes were to be found: the *Carnonacæ* and *Creones*, while the centre of the Highlands was occupied by the *Caledonii*.

Pictish dominance began to be threatened in the sixth century with the first arrival of another Celtic people, the Gaelic Scots from Ireland. The Scots established the kingdom of Dalriada in the area of Argyll in the south-west. The power and influence of the Scots gradually increased by military conquest and through the missionary activity of St Columba of Iona in the sixth century, and then of St Maelrubha of Applecross in the eighth century.

By the time the kingdoms of the Scots and Picts were united in 844 under Kenneth MacAlpin, another wave of immigrants had made their presence felt. The Norse Vikings first came to Scotland to pillage and destroy, but they later established settlements in the Western Isles and northern mainland. For a time in the late ninth century the territory of Thorstein the Red, a royal son of Olaf of Dublin and his curiously named wife, Aud the Deep-Minded, extended from Caithness and eastern Sutherland as far south as Easter Ross. But Thorstein was killed by the Scots and his death marked the beginning of Norse decline. The Scots became dominant and Gaelic became the principal language, and remained so until it was challenged by Scots-English from the twelfth century onwards. However the old Gaelic tongue was still widely

ABOVE: *The scenes carved on the Pictish slab cross from Cadboll (now in the Museum of Antiquities in Edinburgh) show the high level of civilization among the early people of the region. Later legend associated the Pictish stones with the origin of the O'Beolain Earls of Ross; they were supposed to commemorate the brothers of Beolain's Norse bride.*
OPPOSITE: *King Malcolm IV (right) with his grandfather David I portrayed on the twelfth-century charter of Kelso Abbey. In 1162 King Malcolm created his old adversary Malcolm MacEth, Earl of Ross.*

spoken in Easter Ross in the nineteenth century.

Vestiges of these early inhabitants can still be seen in the vicinity of Balnagown. Most memorable are the enigmatic carved Pictish standing stones of Cadboll, Nigg and Shandwick, dating from around the turn of the ninth century. But evidence of the region's early history also survives in place names: Pitcalnie has the characteristic '*pit-*' prefix indicating that it was a Pictish settlement, while Tain and Dingwall take their names from the Norse (*thing* meaning 'assembly'). Balnagown is a Gaelic name meaning the *baile* ('farming township') of the smiths, perhaps an indication that iron ore was once smelted here. The name Ross is also probably of Gaelic origin: *ros* means 'headland' or 'promontory'.

What was the Clan Ross, and how did it come to be associated with Balnagown? For an answer we must go back to a period before the castle was built.

Most Scottish clans take their name from a person. The Clan Ross is unusual since its name is derived from a region: the land of Ross existed before the clan. When the name Ross first appears in history, in the eleventh century, it seems to have applied only to what is now called Easter Ross, between the Beauly Firth, near Inverness, and the Dornoch Firth, together with the inland area along the eastward-flowing rivers. When the official boundaries of Ross-shire were laid down in 1661, the county extended from the east coast across the breadth of Scotland to the Western Isles. This was essentially the territory once held by the mighty Earls of Ross.

The Earls of Ross and the Beginnings of the Clan Ross

THE FIRST ROSS CHIEFS of Balnagown derived their name, much of their land and their prestige from their ancestors, the Earls of Ross, who wielded great power in the Highlands during the middle ages, before their title was taken from them by the king. The power of the great northern lords had always caused anxiety to the Scottish kings.

For three centuries after 844 the royal dynasty established by Kenneth MacAlpin struggled to establish its authority throughout Scotland. It faced considerable opposition in the north-east and south-west from powerful local chiefs. Such magnates were called mormaers, the Gaelic equivalent of Norse jarls, or English earls.

The mormaer of Ross first appears in history in the early twelfth century. This was a time when King David I was attempting to quell the ambitions of Angus, mormaer of Moray, the most powerful of the northern chiefs and a rival for the throne. Among Angus's allies was another chief, Malcolm MacEth, whose family had become mormaers of Ross, when Ross, which had previously been part of Moray, became a separate entity in the eleventh century.

Angus was killed in 1130, and Malcolm joined forces with another powerful rebel, Somerled of Argyll, but in 1134 he was captured by the king and imprisoned for twenty-eight years at Roxburgh. When he was finally released in 1162, David's grandson, Malcolm IV, restored him to his Ross patrimony, making him the Earl of Ross. The king evidently thought that MacEth's days of rebellion were over. Significantly, however, he made sure that the earldom did not pass to MacEth's son. When Malcolm MacEth died in 1168, the earldom was retained by the king, and it is not until over fifty years later that the next Earl of Ross is recorded.

The rebellious region of Moray and Ross remained a constant irritation to Malcolm IV's successor, William the Lion, as the MacEths and the mormaers of Moray continued to reject his royal authority. William fought several campaigns in an effort to pacify the region, and built a number of castles there, but his young son, Alexander II, still faced further serious rebellion there when he came to the throne in 1214.

The man responsible for quashing at last the ambitions of the MacEths and the mormaers of Moray was a Highland chief from the west, Farquhar MacTaggart. He decisively defeated the rebels, who included Malcolm MacEth's grandsons, in June 1215 and presented the king with the bloodied heads of the leaders. Suitably impressed, Alexander granted him a knighthood, and not long afterwards (the precise date is uncertain) created him Earl of Ross.

OPPOSITE: *A view near Applecross on the west coast. Here lay the ancestral lands of Farquhar MacTaggart, the founder of the O'Beolain dynasty of Earls of Ross in the thirteenth century.*

ABOVE: *The south transept of Fearn Abbey, where Earl Farquhar, the monastery's founder, is buried, is now a roofless ruin.*

TOP AND OPPOSITE: *In recent years the Clan Wallace has recreated something of the authentic character of medieval clans, which has often been overlaid by nineteenth-century sentimentality.*

His loyalty to the king and his military skill were again required in 1235 when another rebellion broke out in Galloway. Alexander II led his army there to put down the rebels, but his men were attacked by the Galwegians while they were pitching camp. Farquhar arrived late and saved the day, attacking the rebels from the rear and routing them.

Farquhar MacTaggart was a native Gael. His origins lay in the west, in what was then part of Argyll, where his family were hereditary 'lay abbots' of Applecross, possessing the extensive lands of the defunct abbey of St Maelrubha. This seems to be the explanation for Farquhar's curious patronymic, MacTaggart or, in its more authentic Gaelic form, *mac an t-sagart*, which means 'son of the priest'.

Like most Celtic dynasties, Farquhar's family claimed descent from an illustrious ancestor, in their case a Celtic chief called Beolain and his Norse wife. It was said that she had been traded in marriage by her Viking father in return for permission to take home booty. Her brothers had sailed from Norway to reclaim her but had perished when their ship was wrecked. Later, the Pictish standing stones in Easter Ross were said to be their memorials.

In the thirteenth century the O'Beolain Earls of Ross were unusual among the northern earls. They were native Highlanders, whereas most of the local magnates were of foreign extraction, placed there by the Scottish kings in order to break the power of the old dynasties established in the region. Earldoms were given to members of the Comyn family from Normandy and to the Flemish Freskin family. Farquhar married his son and heir William to a daughter of William Comyn, Earl of Buchan, and his daughter Euphemia to one of the Freskin family, Sir Walter de Moravia (Moray). Another daughter, Christina, is said to have married Olaf, the Norse King of Man.

As he became part of this network of family alliances, Farquhar, the Highland chief, was entering the feudal world of international courtly society. Thus we find him in 1237 visiting the English Court to witness a diplomatic agreement, and in 1244 he was a member of an embassy of Scottish nobles sent to Rome to inform the Pope of Scotland's peace treaty with England.

It was during an early visit to the English court that, according to one story, Farquhar distinguished himself in a wrestling match with a French courtier, and, having vowed that he would found a monastery if he was victorious, duly established an abbey in Easter Ross in 1225. The abbey, manned by canons of the French order of Prémontré, moved to its present site at Fearn (four miles east of Balnagown) in 1238. Its founder, the first and greatest of the O'Beolain line of Earls, died in 1251 and was buried in the abbey. The site of his tomb can still be seen in a roofless side-chapel. Many of the later Rosses were to find their last resting places in the family vault at Fearn.

Earl Farquhar's reputation was embellished by later generations. Robert Bain in his *History of Ross* remarks sceptically that Farquhar 'is credited by the Clan and other annalists with quite a number of achievements of the Munchausen

ABOVE: *Ballone Castle, near Tarbat Ness, is said to have been one of the strongholds of the medieval Earls of Ross. A nineteenth-century print shows the ruins of the later tower-house built in the mid-sixteenth century.*

order', but it is beyond doubt that he was the most powerful and successful Highland leader of his day.

The great lords of northern and western Scotland in the thirteenth century, and for some centuries to come, played a double part, in that they were both feudal barons and tribal chiefs. As vassals of the king they owed their sovereign the allegiance due to a feudal overlord, but their hold over the people living in their territory was based on a different sort of relationship. This relationship was to remain the distinguishing characteristic of the

clan system until the power of the clans was broken in the eighteenth century. As Sir Fitzroy Maclean has written: 'In its ancient form the clan was founded on the deeply-rooted Celtic principle of kindness, a mixture of kinship and tradition, stronger than any written law.'

The emergence of the clan system in the middle ages and early modern times followed the destruction of the old Celtic dynasties in the north but it preserved ancient Celtic practices and attitudes.The Romantic vision of the Highland clans which has developed since the cult of Scotland in the nineteenth century, with its clearly defined clan maps and tartans, can be misleading. In fact, clans were always more varied and flexible than the nineteenth-century image would suggest. They were generally large groups held together by a sense of common kinship, obeying one overall chief and with an attachment to a particular stretch of territory. Absolute power lay with the chief. Chiefdom was hereditary and smaller branches of the clan (later called 'septs') were headed by members of junior branches of the chief's family. In general, a clansman's loyalty was first to the Chief of his clan, second to his branch of the clan, third to the clan, and fourth to the sovereign.

The chief dispensed justice to his clansmen, granted them their land and controlled all aspects of their lives. He offered them protection and was duty-bound to seek revenge for a harm inflicted on a member of the clan. In return, whenever the chief sent out the fiery cross as a signal for the clan to rally, the clansmen had an absolute duty to answer his call. The strength of a clan was directly related to the prestige of the chief, and above all on the amount of land he held and the number of men that land could support. The survival of a clan depended on the survival of its chiefs as landholders and loss of land could result in a drift of supporters to another chief. Today the spirit of kinship among the Rosses is kept alive by Clan Ross associations throughout the world, but the old life-or-death power of the chiefs is no more.

On becoming Earl of Ross (the First Earl of the new line), Farquhar had been granted the territories that had been held by the MacEths. His own lands were now added to these and he also received other grants from the king. Henceforth the heartland of the O'Beolain Earls and of their heirs, the clan chiefs and lairds of Balnagown, was to be in the east, on the peninsula south of Dornoch Firth. The clan which the successors of Farquhar led took its name not from MacTaggart or Beolain, but from the land of Ross, though scholars have suggested that Gaelic name *Siol Gille Andrias* ('the clan of the companions of Andrew'), which seems to be synonymous with the Clan Ross, is derived from some long-forgotten ancestor.

ABOVE: *The Ross arms were adopted not only by the descendants of the Earls, but also by the Lairds of Balnagown who succeeded them. They appear, for instance, in the decoration of the mid-nineteenth century Dining Room at the castle.*

BELOW: *The Ross coat of arms, with its three lions rampant, first appears on the seals of the thirteenth-century Earls of Ross. This is an impression of the seal of William, the Third Earl (1274-1322) and bears the inscription: S. [= seal] WILLELMI COMITIS DE ROS.*

OPPOSITE: *The later Lairds of Balnagown were descendants of Sir William Wallace, through Elizabeth, the wife of Admiral Sir John Lockhart Ross, who inherited Wallace's estate at Lamington from her mother, Henrietta Baillie. According to tradition, the ancient wooden chair now in the hall at Balnagown belonged to the great Scottish patriot.*

The continental newcomers in the twelfth and thirteenth centuries were able to establish a Celtic sense of kinship with their people, just as the native chiefs had. And western Highland chiefs, such as the O'Beolain Earls of Ross and their kinsmen the Mackenzies of Kintail, were able to establish themselves in the east, once they acquired land there. After the fifteenth century, when the Mackenzies, formerly vassals of the O'Beolains, took over much of the old earldom's territory, the inhabitants seem easily to have switched their allegiance to their new chiefs and become Mackenzies.

For four generations after Farquhar the earldom remained with the male line of the O'Beolain family. The earls did not reside at Balnagown (the castle was not yet built), but they are known to have lived nearby. Many of the castles in the vicinity were in the possession of the Earls at various times. Sometimes they resided at Dingwall, in the royal castle granted by Alexander II to Farquhar, and later granted to Farquhar's grandson by King Robert the Bruce. Ballone Castle on the cliffs near Tarbat Ness is also said to have been theirs. But their principal seat seems to have been Delny Castle, where the Third and Fifth Earls, as well as Farquhar himself, are known to have died. Nothing today remains of the castle at Delny, which was situated just three miles south-west of Balnagown.

Farquhar's son, William, who became Second Earl on his father's death, seems to have inherited his father's military prowess. His marriage into the Comyn family, then the most powerful family in Scotland, was significant. When the Comyns, concerned about King Alexander III's rapprochement with England, made their own treaty with Prince Llywelyn of Wales, Earl William was one of the signatories. However, it was as a loyal servant of King Alexander, that the Earl laid waste the Isle of Skye in 1262 as part of Alexander's campaign to break Norse power in the Western Isles. A year later he was prominent in the defeat inflicted at the Battle of Largs on the army sent by King Haakon IV of Norway in

OPPOSITE: *King Robert the Bruce, a seventeenth-century portrait by George Jamesone. The enmity between the Earls of Ross and the Bruces ended in 1308 when the Third Earl recognized Robert as King and married his son to Bruce's sister.*

retaliation. His exploits were mentioned in the Icelandic *Haakon Saga*. When, in 1266 the Western Isles finally came under the Scottish crown, Earl William was rewarded with the title of Lord of Skye and Lewis, a further extension of Ross power.

The career of William, the Third Earl, who succeeded his father in 1274, illustrates the difficulties faced by the Scottish magnates in the succession crisis which followed the unexpected death of Alexander III in 1284 and that of his granddaughter and sole heir, Margaret, the 'Maid of Norway' in 1290. The crisis gave King Edward I of England the opportunity to intervene in Scottish affairs and claim his overlordship of the country. Like other nobles, William paid homage to Edward in 1291 and was a supporter of John Balliol, the English-backed candidate for the throne. But in 1296, when hostilities broke out between Scotland and England, he took part in the Scottish attack across the border which ended in Edward's victory over the Scottish army at Dunbar. The Earl was among those captured and spent six years in the custody of the English court. During this time William Wallace and Andrew Murray fought on against English domination and upheld the cause of Scottish independence. But with her husband held hostage in London it is not surprising that the Earl's wife, Euphemia, helped crush this Scottish resistance in Moray.

The leaders of Scottish resistance to Edward I, such as Wallace and Murray, were mostly younger sons with little to lose; a great magnate such as the Earl of Ross played a different game to keep control of his lands and power. On his release in 1303, with his son left behind at the English court to ensure his good conduct. Earl William remained obedient to Edward and even accepted from him the office of 'Warden beyond the Spey'. In 1305 he violated the sanctuary of St Duthac at Tain by seizing there the wife and daughter of Robert the Bruce and delivering them to the English King. Family loyalty no doubt also played a part in the Earl's opposition to Bruce. After all, William's mother was a Comyn, and in his ruthless removal of rivals to the throne Bruce had brutally murdered John Comyn, Earl of Buchan, not long before. By 1307 Bruce had consolidated

ROBERTVS BRVSIVS
Anno · 1306

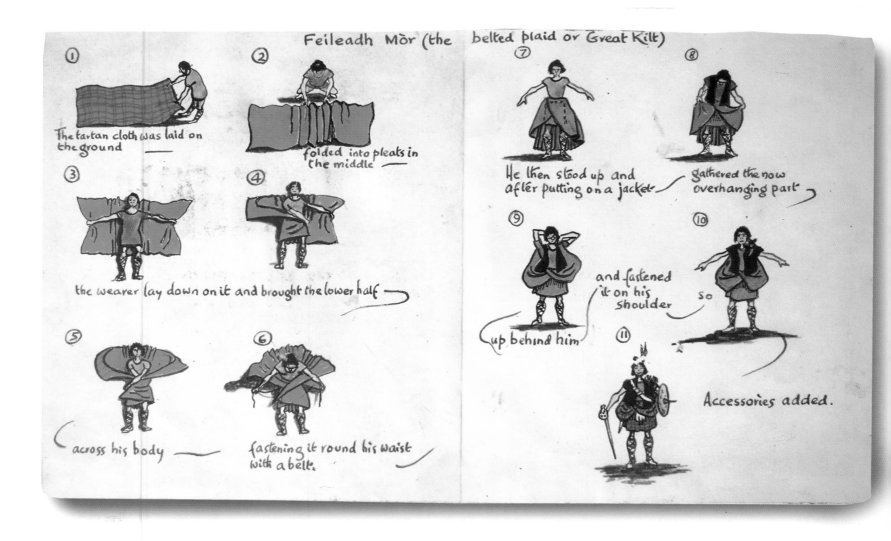

Feileadh Mòr (the belted plaid or Great Kilt)

① The tartan cloth was laid on the ground

② folded into pleats in the middle

③ the wearer lay down on it and brought the lower half

④

⑤ across his body

⑥ fastening it round his waist with a belt.

⑦ He then stood up and after putting on a jacket

⑧ gathered the now overhanging part

⑨ up behind him

and fastened it on his shoulder

⑩ so

⑪ Accessories added.

ABOVE: The traditional Highland kilt. An eighteenth-century English observer noted with distaste: '. . . for the most part the petticoat is so short that in a windy day, going up a hill or stooping, the indecency of it is plainly discovered.'

his power and advanced up the Great Glen to invade Ross. With no help from England forthcoming, Earl William abandoned his former position, called a truce and in 1308 did homage to Bruce. His submission and the realignment of his allegiance, was sealed by the marriage of Hugh, his son and heir, to Bruce's sister, Maud.

Until his death in 1322, the Earl continued to support the Scottish cause. He led the men of Ross in Bruce's army at Bannockburn in 1314, and he was one of the nobles who signed the most famous document in Scottish history, the Declaration of Arbroath of 1320, which laid the foundations of Scottish liberty and independence.

Hugh, the Fourth Earl, as has been seen, spent time at the English court, where he was sent as a hostage in 1303 to ensure his father's good conduct back in Scotland. As the brother-in-law of King Robert the Bruce, he is said to have intended to build a castle at Balnagown which would express the Earldom's current high status. His death on 19 July 1333 prevented this. Hugh was one of the five Scottish earls slain at the Battle of Halidon Hill near Berwick, when Edward III's English army inflicted a devastating defeat on the Scots. Although he was wearing the miraculous shirt of St Duthac, which was supposed to protect its wearer from harm, Hugh was pierced in the throat by an English arrow. The shirt was removed from his body by the English, who returned it with due reverence to the saint's shrine at Tain.

William, the Fifth Earl, Hugh's son, was never on good terms with his sovereign and cousin, King David II (1329-71), Robert the Bruce's son. In 1346, when the king was mustering his forces at Perth for the invasion of England, the Earl withdrew his men and returned to Ross following the murder in Elcho abbey of his kinsman by marriage, Ronald Mac Ruairi of the Isles. The finger of guilt pointed clearly at the Earl and it is clear that by his hasty departure he hoped to escape royal retribution. Further royal mistrust was created after the invasion had failed and the King was taken captive by the English. The Earl and his half-brother Hugh were among the magnates who showed little enthusiasm for contributing to the payment of his large ransom.

Earl William's seems to have been principally interested in his possessions in the western Highlands and islands. He was married to a daughter of Angus, Lord of the Isles, and was one of a powerful group of Highland lords whom King David came to regard as a serious threat to his authority. They included Robert the Steward (who was married to William's sister, another Euphemia), John of the Isles, John of Lorne and Gillespic Campbell. After the king returned from imprisonment in 1357, the Earl was one of those who 'contumaciously absented' themselves from his Parliaments in 1366 and 1367. When the King was finally in a position to subdue his dangerous magnates, he did so ruthlessly. The Earl of Ross was one of the last to suffer. In 1370, shortly before David's death, the King forced the Earl to resign all his lands to the crown and receive them back under a new charter which made the earldom heritable in the female line. The Earl's only surviving child, also called Euphemia, now became the heiress. In 1365, she had married Sir Walter Leslie, who had already been granted some

of the Earldom's lands. After David II's death the Earl protested that he had granted the lands under duress, 'on account of the rigour of the same lord king and by fear of his wrath'. But his protests were in vain.

When Earl William died in 1372 at Delny, Euphemia, with her husband Leslie, succeeded to the Earldom. It later went through various vicissitudes, passing by marriage to the Macdonald family and was finally annexed to the crown in 1476, when John Macdonald, Earl of Ross and Lord of the Isles, was deprived of the title. Henceforth it was to be reserved for the second son of the King of Scotland: the present Earl of Ross is Prince Andrew, Duke of York.

Some later Lairds of Balnagown and leaders of the Clan Ross were convinced that the royal seizure of the title in the fourteenth and fifteenth centuries was illegal; they believed that they had good grounds to claim the ancient earldom for themselves.

Balnagown

Edinburgh

Earldom of Ross Clan Ross territory c.1600

ABOVE: *The ruins of St Duthac's Chapel. In the middle ages the saint's relics, which had returned to Tain from Armagh in 1253, were kept in the care of a hermit.*

Hugh of Rarichies and the Early Lairds of Balnagown

WHEN THE EARLDOM was taken from the male line of the O'Beolain family on the death of Earl William in 1372, the allegiance of the clan did not go with it but passed to his half-brother, Hugh of Rarichies, who took his name from the villages of Easter and Wester Rarichie. According to most reckonings Hugh is regarded as the first true Chief of the Clan Ross.

Hugh had some reason to be disappointed with his inheritance. At one time he himself had hoped to become Earl of Ross. In 1350, William had intended to make him the heir presumptive to the earldom if his son William died, but the King had withheld his consent to this and twenty years later had taken the earldom away from the male line of the family. Hugh made sure that his family's connection with the old earldom was not forgotten by taking Ross as his surname. This sense of grievance lingered with the clan: in the early eighteenth century the then Laird of Balnagown, David Ross, argued that the earldom had been taken unjustly, and in 1778 Munro Ross of Pitcalnie took the case to the House of Lords, though no judgment is recorded.

Hugh Ross had not been left empty-handed: Earl William had granted his half-brother some important property. To add to the lands of Wester and Easter Rarichie, which he had been granted by his father, Hugh had received in 1350 the lands of Balnagown (from which his descendants were named), Achahaynitt and Gortie. The grant was confirmed by a charter of King David II before he died, and in 1375, a year after Hugh's death, King Robert II (1371-90), who was married to Hugh's sister Euphemia, set his seal to a Charter of Confirmation by which he 'approved, ratified, and . . . confirmed that gift and grant which the late William Earl of Ross made . . . to the late Hugh Ross (Hugoni de Ross) his brother of the lands of Balnegoun [etc.]. . . to be held . . . by William Ross, son and heir of the said late Hugh Ross'. A replica of the charter is displayed today in the Trophy Room at the castle.

The heirs of **Hugh, First Laird of Balnagown**, were not the mighty magnates that their ancestors, the Earls, had been. They acted on a smaller stage without the same influence over national affairs. Nevertheless, as lairds they wielded considerable power in their domains, and through dynastic marriages or by brute force, they managed to extend their lands. In the fifteenth century the clan was one of the strongest in the Highlands. At this time the chiefs briefly and unsuccessfully sought to regain their ancestral strength in the Western Isles, but from now on their effective power lay in the northern part of Easter Ross. Their heartland was the territory to the north and west of Balnagown.

The descendants of Hugh of Rarichies were to remain the lairds here for over three hundred years, until the line failed with the death in 1711 of the Thirteenth Laird. The Ross Lairds of Balnagown were a fiery dynasty, frequently embroiled in clan quarrels and dubious adventures. In the end their lawlessness during the turmoil of the sixteenth century helped bring them near to ruin.

ABOVE: *The seal of Queen Euphemia, sister of Hugh of Rarichies, who married as her second husband the Earl of Strathearn, the future King Robert II.*

OPPOSITE: *The west front of Balnagown. This is the oldest part of the castle and incorporates the structure of the early tower-house.*

ABOVE: *William Ross, the son of Hugh of Rarichies, the first true Chief of the Clan Ross and first Laird of Balnagown, received royal confirmation of his possession of Balnagown in a charter of King Robert II in 1375.*

No firm date can be given for the building of the earliest castle at Balnagown. As we have seen, the name suggests that this was an old settlement. It is likely that, if a building did stand on the site in Hugh's time, it was a far humbler structure than the late-fifteenth-century tower-house which forms the core of the present castle. No doubt some sort of building would have been erected here between Hugh's acquisition of the lands around 1350 and the earliest recorded mention of the castle in 1490.

The site, near the old stronghold of the Earls of Ross at Delny, was well placed. It stood near the main road from the south to Tain, and to the north and east it was protected by the steep banks down to the Balnagown River. Unlike the castles built in the region by King William the Lion, Balnagown was not a strategic base for the domination of a wide area. It was built as a laird's fortified residence, a place of safety, guarding his fertile land nearby, to be defended against attack when necessary.

The first generations that followed Hugh of Rarichies are a shadowy group. What little information we can glean from the records and chronicles indicates a family increasing in wealth and power, intermarrying with powerful newcomers and with the highest aristocracy of the region.

Confirmed in his possession of the Balnagown estates by King Robert II's charter of 1375, **William Ross, the Second Laird**, called Crunblache, was succeeded by his son **Walter Ross, the Third Laird**, known as Walter Cluganach ('of the Earring'). He made an adroit marriage in 1398 to Catherine, the daughter of Paul Mactyre, an infamous freebooter. Mactyre, who claimed descent from the Norwegian Kings of Man, had acquired a vast fortune in the northern Highlands mainly through extortion. In *Ane Breve Cronicle of the Erllis of Ross* (a sixteenth-century manuscript history now on loan from Balnagown to the Tain Museum) he is described as 'a very takand [taking] man', meaning a man who had taken much for himself. His daughter brought as part of her dowry the lands of Strathoykel, Strathcarron and Freevater; the Balnagown estates were thus greatly extended to the north and west.

According to the same Breve Cronicle, **Hugh Ross, the Fourth Laird**, who succeeded his father in 1412, made an advantageous marriage to Janet, a daughter of the Earl of Sutherland, the Rosses' powerful neighbour to the north (though there seems to be no record of this marriage in the Sutherland family records).

John Ross, the Fifth Laird, who had married in 1456 a daughter of Torquil MacLeod of Lewis, had ambitions to regain some of the lands of his ancestors the Earls when the Earldom was broken up in 1476. He grandly called himself 'Lord John of the Isles', but made little headway in his attempt to win Hebridean territory.

The marriage alliance with the Macleods of Lewis reinforced the clan rivalry between the Rosses and the Mackays, since the Macleods had long been bitter enemies of the Mackays. The feud with the Mackays resulted in one of the greatest disasters ever to hit the Clan Ross, in which **Alexander Ross, the Sixth Laird** was slain along with many of his men.

The sequence of events is a good example of the violence and brutality of blood feud between clans. In 1487 a band of Rosses burned to death a group of Mackays who had sought refuge in Tarbat church, a few miles east of Balnagown. Bound by the code of clan honour to seek vengeance for this atrocity, the Chief of the Mackays was driven to ask for assistance from the Earl of Sutherland, although the Sutherlands were traditional enemies of the Mackays. The combined force entered Strathoykel and laid waste the Ross country with fire and sword. Alexander Ross mustered his clansmen and battle was joined at Alt na Charrais in Strathcarron. Among those killed in the fierce encounter were the Ross Chief and seventeen of his most important followers, the leading landowners of Ross. It took many years for the clan to recover from this calamity.

With the clan in disarray, Alexander's widow, Dorothy, who was a Sutherland by birth, took measures to safeguard the family property. She is said to have ordered two of her henchmen to save the treasure by burying it. When their task was completed they were given poisoned drinks by their mistress, who never divulged the hiding place. The whereabouts of the treasure are still unknown, but it is believed by some to be concealed near Balnagown.

It was in 1490 during the time of Dorothy's son, **David Ross, the Seventh Laird**, that we find the earliest documentary evidence for a castle at Balnagown. No doubt, after the disaster at Alt na Charrais it was thought prudent to improve defences. David is reported to have undertaken building work using rubble stone gathered

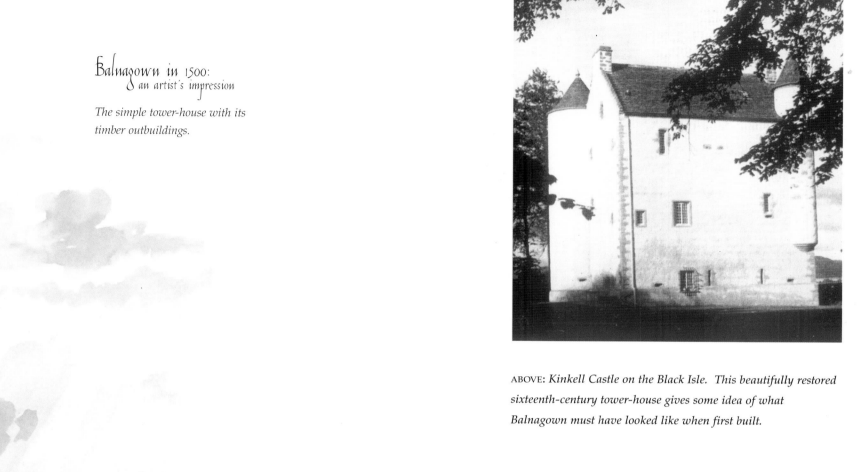

Balnagown in 1500: an artist's impression

The simple tower-house with its timber outbuildings.

ABOVE: *Kinkell Castle on the Black Isle. This beautifully restored sixteenth-century tower-house gives some idea of what Balnagown must have looked like when first built.*

from the estate. This was probably the first stone-built tower-house at Balnagown, which is the earliest part of today's castle.

The tower, which forms the nucleus of the western end of the present building, was typical of many such tower-houses built throughout Scotland in this period. In a world of clan feuds and petty warfare a laird's house had to be defended. Scottish tower-houses were never sophisticated military architecture. As the architectural historian John Dunbar has observed, their 'defensive qualities . . . were entirely passive, reliance being placed upon the limitation of the ground area to a minimum, and upon the construction of thick outer walls bound together horizontally by one or more barrel-vaults'.

Balnagown was the simplest type of tower-house: built on a rectangular plan with accommodation arranged vertically on several storeys. The vaulted rooms on the ground floor would have been used as servants' quarters and storerooms. On occasion these secure rooms could also be used as dungeons for detaining those who had incurred the displeasure of the clan chief.

Entry to the castle was at first-floor level by means of a turnpike (spiral) stair, with a ground-floor entrance door. The first floor was the principal storey comprising the laird's hall (the room now called the Trophy Room), the laird's private audience room where clan business was transacted and the laird entertained his guests. It was not a 'great hall' for communal gatherings of the clan; such halls were generally separate structures, not part of tower-houses. Above the laird's hall were the living and sleeping quarters for his family and guests, with access to the roof.

The roof and the ceiling of the hall were constructed of beams made from whole tree trunks, and the height of the trees determined the width of the building. Originally the roof covering would have been thatch.

The exterior of the rubble walls would have been harled (roughcast with small gravel and lime), as was customary in Scotland. The fashion for stripping buildings to reveal the rubble stone beneath dates from the nineteenth century when rough masonry was thought to be more romantically picturesque. At Balnagown the pink harling has been reinstated in the latest restoration.

The massive boulders used as foundations ensured that the castle would endure, and the great thickness of the walls and the vaulted ground floor provided some protection against the danger of fire; flaming torches were often hurled when castles were attacked.

The loopholes in the lower storey were for shooting at attackers, and also provided ventilation. By the later sixteenth century such loopholes had become more decorative, or symbolic, than practical. During the recent restoration of this part of the castle these gun-loopholes have been uncovered and retained. The building could not have survived attack by artillery, but before the development of such weapons tower-houses could be practically impregnable.

Adjacent to the tower-house, and surrounded by a defensive wall, smaller, humbler buildings arranged around a small

courtyard would have provided accommodation for retainers, horses and cattle. There would also have been a bakehouse and brewery to supply the castle.

The small windows were unglazed, the rooms were lit by smoky torches and plumbing was rudimentary. The floor of the laird's hall

was strewn with rushes, and its walls were unplastered. Over the following centuries, as defence became less of a priority, and the castle's inhabitants came to expect greater levels of comfort, the building was modified and extended, but the west wing still hints at its original austere and forbidding appearance.

ABOVE: *The Trophy Room photographed in 1958. Originally this was the laird's hall, the reception room for the Chiefs of the Clan Ross. It is the oldest part of the castle, though much altered since it was first built in the late fifteenth century.*

JACOBVS · D · GRATIA
REX · SCOTORVM

The Sixteenth Century: Troublesome Lairds and Incompetent Witches

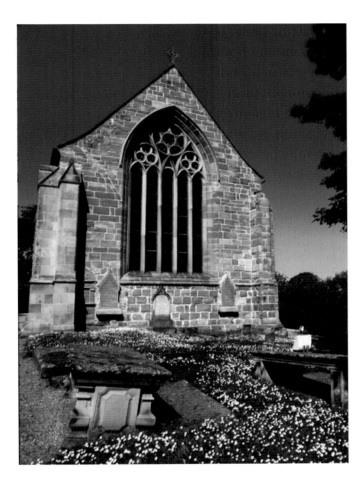

TOP: *The Collegiate Church at Tain was founded by William, Earl of Ross in 1321. Two and a half centuries later it was despoiled by his descendant, Alexander Ross of Balnagown.*

ABOVE: *Seen through the archway of the King's Bridge, the North front of the castle looks forbidding.*

OPPOSITE: *A contemporary portrait of King James IV. He often took the road past Balnagown, across the King's Bridge and along the King's Causeway, on his way to St Duthac's shrine at Tain.*

IN RETROSPECT THE REIGN of King James IV (1488-1513), seemed a golden age. Scotland's economy was thriving. On the throne was a popular and successful monarch, a Renaissance ruler surrounded by a brilliant and cultured cosmopolitan court. The King often passed near Balnagown on his regular pilgrimages to St Duthac's shrine at Tain. The blessings of the saint were not the only incentive for the King's journeys to Tain; his mistress Janet Kennedy, whose son he made Earl of Moray, lived at Darnaway, which James would visit en route. The royal entourage would then make their way north, crossing the Balnagown River by the bridge, known as the King's Bridge, just upstream from the castle.

James made his last pilgrimage to Tain in 1513, just before summoning his army to march against the English. The disastrous defeat at Flodden Field that year, when the flower of the Scots nobility were wiped out and James himself was killed fighting in their midst, ushered in a long period of instability in Scotland. The kingdom was convulsed by religious conflict and violent power struggles dominated the long minorities of James V, Mary Queen of Scots and her son, James VI. Not until the early decades of the seventeenth century were stability and order restored.

It is not known why **Sir David Ross, the Seventh Laird of Balnagown**, received a knighthood. The honour was probably procured through the influence of his second wife, Margaret Stewart, daughter of the Duke of Albany, who was Governor of the kingdom during the minority of James V (1516-43). In any case, it marked an increase in status for the Balnagown Rosses.

David died in 1520 and was succeeded by his son **Walter Ross, the Eighth Laird**, whose mother, Helen Keith daughter of the Laird of Inverurie, was remembered as 'ane guid woman'. Walter came to a sudden and inglorious end when he was killed with three of his followers at Tain in 1528 during a skirmish with the MacKays. Their heads were hung from a nearby tree.

Alexander Ross, the Ninth Laird of Balnagown and perhaps the most notorious, was one of those who took advantage of the troubled times. Perhaps Alexander should not be judged too harshly. The feud-ridden world of the Scottish clans had always been violent, and this period is better documented than earlier times and consequently we know more about complaints, lawsuits and official reprimands.

The Laird of Balnagown's misdemeanours pale beside those committed a few years before by Black Andrew Munro, the psychopathic laird of the neighbouring castle of Milton (near where

New Tarbat House now stands), whose murderous reign of terror over his tenantry, many of whom he slaughtered himself or ordered to be buried alive, came to an end with his sudden death around 1520. For his amusement he had ordered the women who had come to gather in the harvest on his land to work stark naked, and as he descended the castle steps to view the spectacle after an ample feast he tripped and broke his neck. (His ghost is said to haunt the area; since the demolition of Milton Castle it appears to have migrated to Balnagown where it occasionally makes its presence felt.)

Alexander Ross did not perpetrate such wanton cruelty, but he was a ruthless bully. We know from a document from the Balnagown archives that in March 1553 he was ordering a shipment of chain-mail coats for his men and 'ane Culvering that beis ryt fyne and schotes fur four ferynks of fyne culvering poudyr . . .' – a reference to an eighteen-pounder cannon 'that is right fine and shoots far', together with the requisite gunpowder. As W. Macgill, the editor of the Balnagown documents, comments: 'In the phrase "that beis right fyne" we can almost hear the Chief gloating over the prospect of it.' In such uncertain time, of course, a laird had to protect his property, but it soon becomes clear that Alexander's intentions were not entirely defensive, as he embarked on a career of destruction and outrage, raiding lands, destroying mansions and exacting rents to which he had no right.

When the Protestant Reformation got underway in Scotland in 1559, Alexander was quick to profit from the destruction of the old Catholic order. The fervour of iconoclasts stirred by John Knox's sermons was turned against the images and relics of saints, and the relics of St Duthac at his shrine at Tain in their precious gold and silver reliquaries were in danger. In 1560, when Nicholas Ross, the Provost of Tain and Abbot of Fearn, was preparing to go to Edinburgh to attend Parliament, he entrusted his kinsman, the Laird of Balnagown, with the relics for safekeeping at the castle. The valuable objects were carefully itemized in a receipt which still survives. They were never seen again. Most probably the laird sold them to raise cash, but

there is a possibility that, like the treasure of Alexander's fifteenth-century namesake, they are hidden somewhere.

There were other outrages: in 1562 some of the canons of Fearn Abbey submitted a formal complaint that Alexander had acquired land from them under duress.

In 1573 his destruction of the castle of Alexander Innes at Cadboll a few miles east of Balnagown finally brought the laird into serious trouble with the authorities. Regent Morton, the ruler of Scotland following the abdication and exile of Mary Queen of Scots, ordered him to Edinburgh, where he was imprisoned in the castle and released only on the promise that he rebuild Cadboll. After his release he submitted a formal complaint, protesting his innocence and alleging that he had been mistreated.

His behaviour was causing his clansmen serious concern. It was desirable to have a strong chief who could exert his authority and raise the prestige of the clan. However, one whose extortionist tactics reduced his tenants to penury and whose outrageous treatment of his neighbours threatened to bring disgrace and expropriation upon the clan was a liability. In 1580 Alexander's tenants complained they were 'so herreit and wrakkit' by their laird that they were unable to pay their taxes, and the Commendator of Fearn wrote of 'barbarous cruelties, injuries and intollerable oppressions and bludesched' committed by the laird on his tenants. A letter of 1577 to Alexander signed by prominent members of the clan (his 'kith and friends') including his son and heir George Ross, urged him to serve God and be 'obedient to authoritie & ye regent . . . rather nor to perish his hous kyn and freinds & tyne the riggis [lose the property] that his elders wan, for the kith & freinds feiris ane stranger to cum in his roume quhilk wilbe to his & thairis uter wrak . . .'

Alexander, however, persisted in his disregard for authority. When he failed to appear to answer 'letters of horning' in 1583, he was duly horned (proclaimed an outlaw, which was traditionally done in Scotland by the blowing of a horn). Letters of fire and sword were issued against him, signed by his son, amongst others. A Decree of

Logy:

Logy   K:

Bar
vills

Knokmoulyn:
Mill

Balnagoun
Castell.

Mills

Meltoun Cast:

ABOVE: *The present King's Bridge, probably dates from the eighteenth century.*

PREVIOUS PAGE: *Thomas Pont's map of Easter Ross, drawn between 1580 and 1590, shows Balnagown together with other castles on the peninsula.*

OPPOSITE: *The enlarged drawing of Balnagown on the map clearly shows the tower-house with its staircase tower. Just to the south of it is Milton (or Milntoun) Castle, home of the notorious 'Black Andrew', whose ghost still haunts the region.*

Arrestment issued in 1586 and preserved in the Trophy Room, records that he was 'alutterlie dischargit of all titill and ryt to the mains and place of Balnagowin . . .' and that, although the castle and lands had officially passed to his son George, Alexander was continuing to levy rents on the property which had been confiscated from him. Surprisingly in 1588 he was still serving as Provost of Tain. He was eventually imprisoned in Tantallon Castle on the Lothian coast, but was released before his death in 1592.

It is not clear whether Alexander was permanently deprived of the lairdship. In 1592 King James VI outlawed the Rosses of Balnagown for harbouring the rebel Earl of Bothwell, who was seeking to assassinate the King. The aged Alexander was still referred to as the laird.

Alexander had not brought the Rosses to utter ruin as his clansmen had prophesied in 1577, but his reckless behaviour had done damage. The financial difficulties which beset the lairds during the seventeenth century seem to have started in his time. But for all his outrageous behaviour, Alexander Ross did not lose his position as a prominent member of the Highland nobility and his family continued to be bound into the tight-knit network of Highland family alliances which had developed over the centuries. His first wife was a Sinclair, daughter of the Earl of Caithness, his second, a Mackenzie, the daughter of the Lord of Kintail and the mother of the first of the Rosses of Pitcalnie.

George Ross, his son by his first wife, became **the Tenth Laird** in 1592. He had received a university education, as demanded by a law passed in James IV's time to raise the literacy and culture of the Scottish landowners. However, his period at St Andrew's seems not to have made him much less reckless and destructive than his father had been. He lived in open feud with his neighbours, laying waste lands, destroying new-sown grass and pasture, stealing cattle, salmon and corn.

Like many Scottish landowners at the turn of the century, the Rosses were finding it hard to live within their means. Serious financial difficulties seem to lie behind the origins of a protracted and confusing dispute between George Ross and his neighbour and kinsman, the Earl of Sutherland, which is documented in the Sutherland papers. In 1583 at Dunrobin Castle, the seat of the Sutherlands, George had arranged a marriage between his son David and the Earl's daughter, Mary Gordon. Not only was the Earl's daughter to receive some of the Balnagown lands, but George also seems to have granted most of the rest of the Balnagown lands to the Earl, as a desperate attempt to raise cash. He must have regretted entering into this agreement and soon started legal proceedings to have the grant of land reversed. The feud between the Rosses of Balnagown and the Gordons of Sutherland was inherited by George's son, and financial problems were to dog Balnagown for the next century.

The Rosses were touched by the witch-hunting craze which swept Scotland and the most of Europe in the sixteenth century and brought the trial and execution of thousands of suspected witches. In 1589 George Ross's younger sister, Katherine, was at the centre of one such trial, which caused a sensation throughout the kingdom. Here the accusations of witchcraft seem to have been incidental; what the case illustrates is the bitterness of family feuds and the apparent ruthlessness of the Balnagown Rosses in seeking to attain their ends.

The case concerned the alleged disposal of inconvenient marriage partners. Katherine Ross was married to Robert Mhor Munro of nearby Foulis Castle, Chief of the Munro Clan, who had a son, Robert, by an earlier marriage. It was alleged that in 1577 Katherine had hatched an outrageous plot to get rid of both her stepson and her sister-in-law, George's wife, Marion. This would free George to marry Marjory, Robert's wife, thus greatly increasing the Balnagown fortunes. And with the stepson out of the way, Katherine's own son could inherit the Munro chiefdom.

Katherine was said to have hired a coven of witches and a wizard from Tain to do the work. The account of their activity suggests extreme incompetence in their craft. One witch made images in butter of the intended victims, took eight shots at them with 'elf arrows' – stone age flint arrowheads which were believed to be of magic origin – missing every time. Another had no more luck with clay images.

The wizard, more practical, was said to have concocted poison, which Katherine administered to George's wife in a dish of kidneys. Marion's death not long afterwards was attributed to this. Robert Munro, however, suffered no harm and the widowed George made a second marriage to someone else. The gang of witches was tried and the wizard burned alive at the stake in November 1577.

Katherine herself was brought to trial thirteen years later, in 1589, after her husband died. His brother Hector had in fact become the new Munro Chief and immediately brought charges against his sister-in-law of complicity in the poisoning and witchcraft. She complained to the Privy Council that the accusation was based 'upoun sinister and wrang informatioun', but she was tried nevertheless. With a jury packed with Rosses and Munros, it was perhaps not surprising that she was acquitted – and immediately brought charges of witchcraft against Hector. The notoriety of Lady Foulis's case added fuel to the witch-hunting craze throughout the country.

While this skulduggery was going on, the

government in Edinburgh was making serious attempts to bring the Highlands to order. The use of weapons was forbidden and lairds were made to send their children to the capital as hostages.

King James VI (later James I of England) assumed direct government of Scotland in 1587. Over the following years he personally sought to persuade the Highland lairds to restore law and order in their territories. Several such letters from the King to George Ross have survived. In 1598, for instance, he urged the laird to act against 'certain our rebellis dwelling within your bounds . . . qlkis for the maist ar yor awin tenentis . . . and in the toun qrof ye ar Provest [i.e. Tain]' who had wrecked and looted a Danish ship on the coast of Ross and 'bring and put thame heir before our justice'.

Often George Ross preferred to use the powers of summary justice given to Highland lairds by the 'Pit and Gallows' Act of 1587, by which they could impose the death penalty on members of their clans – and if the particular guilty clansman could not be found, execute another in his place. Indeed, the Laird of Balnagown was said to be so enthusiastic in this punishment that he was accused of slaughtering his clansmen.

Nonetheless, by the early years of the seventeenth century peace and order had been restored to most of the kingdom. After the removal of his court to London in 1603, James had to remind wayward Scottish lairds of his

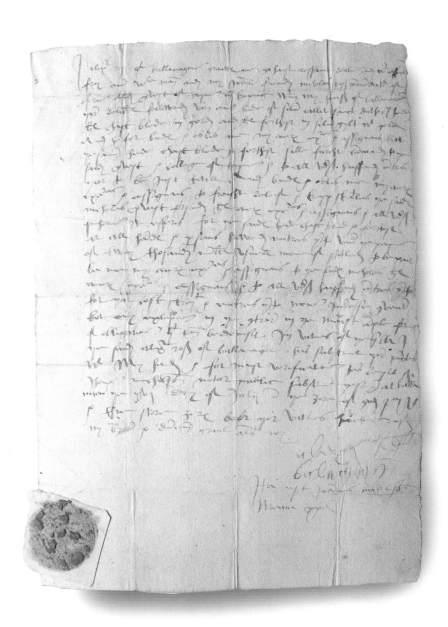

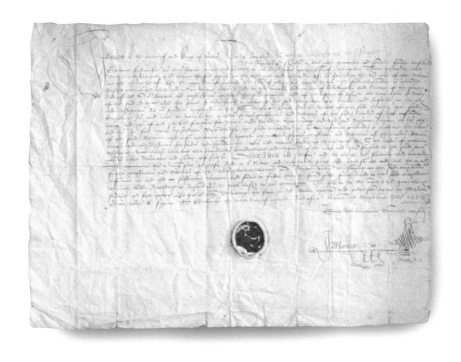

ABOVE: *The receipt for St Duthac's relics which were brought to Balnagown from Tain for safekeeping on 16 July 1560. It is signed and sealed by Alexander Ross and declares that the relics would be 'furcht cumand to the said prevest and college of Tayne and to all uthers heffand entres thrto be just titill' [forthcoming to the said Provost and College of Tain and all others having interest thereto by just title]. The unscrupulous Alexander ignored this promise: the relics and their precious shrine have never been found.*

RIGHT: *A Decree of Arrestment dated April 1586 declaring that the outlawed Alexander Ross had been deprived of Balnagown and its lands. They were given instead to his son George, the Tenth Laird, who proved to be scarcely more law-abiding than his father. The document is now displayed in the Trophy Room.*

authority. This is probably the explanation for the despatch of the royal coat of arms in 1607 by sea from Leith 'for my much honoured and much respected friend the Laird of Balnagowan. . . . Your honour shall be pleased to resave . . . the King's armes, and caus hous them either with iron or timber upon the wall.' The coat of arms was sent, but unfortunately there is no record of where in the castle it was housed.

ABOVE: *The Katherine Ross witch trial was one of many. Shown here is the notorious trial of the North Berwick witches who assisted the rebel Earl of Bothwell. The Balnagown Rosses later sheltered the fugitive Earl.*

OPPOSITE: *King James VI, a portrait by Adrian Vanson painted in 1595, when the king was making successful efforts to end the lawlessness of Highland lairds such as George Ross of Balnagown.*

IACOBVS · 6 · D · G · R
SCOTORVM
ÆTA: 29
1595

The Seventeenth Century: Keeping Up Appearances

ABOVE: *The corner stone at the south-west corner of the tower-house is dated 1600, evidence of extensive alterations at the castle during the lairdship of George Ross.*

OPPOSITE: *A rare glimpse of the castle as it appeared in the late seventeenth and early eighteenth centuries is provided by this portrait of a boy. The seventeenth-century extension had created an L-shaped building with the entrance and staircase in the angle of the 'L'. The French-style turrets and bartizans are decorative features.*

BY THE TIME OF GEORGE ROSS's death in 1615, Balnagown was heavily encumbered with debt, and for the following century the family struggled to escape their financial difficulties. Despite this, the seventeenth-century Rosses of Balnagown concerned themselves with architectural projects and with maintaining their status as clan chiefs.

George Ross had undertaken major building work at the castle. In 1593, James Nicolson, master mason, was paid for 'new wark of Balnagown', probably in connection with the reconstruction and enlargement of the original tower-house. He may have been responsible for the extension of the tower-house northwards, as well as for the bartizan (a small corner turret characteristic of Scottish castles) at the south-east corner and the turret projecting from above the ground floor at the south-west corner. The foundation stone below this turret bears the date 1600.

Martial-looking turrets and bartizans still remained characteristic features of Scottish castles even in these more peaceful times, when in any case the development of artillery meant that such buildings could no longer be effectively defended. The 'rooftop display' of towers and crenellation, which owed something to French models, continued to hold a symbolic significance as an expression of the owner's status. As Sir Robert Ker remarked in 1632, when he advised his son not to remove the battlement from Ancram, it 'makes it look lyk a castle, and hence so nobleste.' A good example of this castellated style is the delightful Castle Stuart near Inverness, built in the 1620s by the 3rd Earl of Moray (the grandfather of Lady Anne, the mistress of Balnagown at the end of the century).

It is not surprising to find building activity at Balnagown at the turn of the seventeenth century. This was the beginning of a building boom throughout Scotland, as the tumult of the previous century gave way to a period of peace.

George's son, **David Ross, the Eleventh Laird of Balnagown**, was more law-abiding than his father or grandfather, and was honoured by having Balnagown made a Barony by James VI. This represented a rise in status. The prominent letter 'B', which appears with the initials of seventeenth-century lairds in the inscriptions in the castle, stands for 'Baron'. However, he also had to confront difficulties to which the recklessness of his predecessors had contributed.

The financial plight of the estate worsened. With creditors pressing for payment and threatening to take his son as security, David successfully petitioned the Privy Council to allow the boy to complete his education at Edinburgh University. It became clear that drastic steps had to be taken to prevent the break-up of the estate. It had to be 'redemit out of the merchandis hand & put into ye freindis hands qa will pay ye merchandis yr wedsets [wadsets, i.e. mortgages] and grant reversions to the barone'. It was thus in the early decades of the seventeenth century that the Laird of Balnagown first seems to have turned to Lord Ross of Halkhead to relieve the financial burden on his estates. By 1622 James, the Fourth Lord Ross, was already in possession of a great stretch of Balnagown lands. This was to have far-reaching consequences.

The Halkhead Rosses were Lowlanders from the west. Their seat was near Paisley, in Renfrewshire. Although they shared the Ross name, their Norman ancestors had come from Yorkshire and were in no way related to the Highland clan. Yet as they sought to extend their property and influence in Ross-shire, they came to cherish hopes of claiming for themselves the ancient Earldom of Ross.

But for the time being Balnagown remained the residence of the descendants of Hugh of Rarichies. When the Eleventh Laird died in 1632 and was buried in the family vault at Fearn Abbey, he was succeeded by his son, another **David, the Twelfth Laird**, who earned a reputation as a valiant soldier, though he vacillated during the Civil Wars. In 1638 he signed the National Covenant against royal intervention in Scottish church affairs, and answered the call of the Marquis of Montrose to join the Covenanters' army, but he then seems to have switched to the Royalist side. In 1650 he was back with the Covenanters, assisting in the final defeat of Montrose (now a Royalist) at Carbisdale. Yet the following year he showed his rejection of Oliver Cromwell's republican Commonwealth and demonstrated his loyalty to the Stuarts.

In 1651 King Charles II was proclaimed King in Edinburgh and summoned his loyal subjects to help him regain his English throne. The King's letter to the Laird of Balnagown is displayed in the Trophy Room. David himself mustered his clan and took part in the lightning march southwards. He fought at the Battle of Worcester, where Charles's Scottish army met humiliating defeat. Two thousand of the King's followers were killed and eight thousand captured, many of them to be sold in slavery in the American colonies. David was captured and stripped of his clan regalia on the battlefield, before being imprisoned at Windsor Castle and the Tower of London, where he died in 1653. He was buried in Westminster Abbey.

On top of the expense that had been incurred in raising and equipping the regiment of eight hundred men, the lands of Balnagown estates now suffered punitive measures from Cromwell's Commonwealth government. However, the exiled King Charles did not forget David Ross's loyalty: after his Restoration to the throne in 1660 he settled an annual pension of £200 on David's son, a third David.

There is evidence that alterations to the castle were made in the time of the Twelfth Laird. A carved dormer pediment, now concealed beneath the roof at the north-east corner of the older part of the castle, bears the date 1651 and the initials of Baron David Ross and his wife Mary Fraser, the eldest daughter of Hugh, Lord Fraser of Lovat. It seems, however, to have been left to their son to undertake more extensive building work.

David Ross, the Thirteenth Laird, the last Balnagown Chief of the Clan Ross, was only nine years old when his father died in London. During his minority the affairs of the estate were handled by his cousin David Ross of Pitcalnie, who was next in seniority in the Clan.

Throughout his life the Thirteenth Laird was beset by financial crises: he lived in constant dread of being arrested for debt. He married a strong-minded and intelligent

Es ist ein Starckes dauerhafftigs Volck behilfft sich mit geringer speiß hatt es nicht brodt so Essen sie Würtzeln, Wans auch die Notturfft erfordert Können sie des Tages Uber die 20 Teutscher meilweges lauffen. haben neben Musqueden Jhre Bogen vnd Köcher vnd Lange Messer.

TOP: *Fearsome Scottish Highland mercenaries portrayed in a seventeenth-century German print. The fighting skills of the Highlanders were valued throughout Europe.*

RIGHT: *Turrets and bartizans remained important features of Scottish castle architecture long after their defensive function had ceased. This bartizan once marked the south-east corner of the building, but now forms part of the south front.*

Balnagown in 1690:
an artist's impression

The original tower-house has been extended with a new wing on the north side

wife, Lady Anne Stewart, the sister of Alexander, Earl of Moray. She exerted a powerful influence over her husband who, although he well liked, was regarded as a weak character and something of a figure of fun. Nevertheless, he did hold public office. As a supporter of the Revolution of 1688, which removed King James VII (James II of England) from the throne, he was made Sheriff of Ross and Governor of Inverness by King William III, and had to organize the defence of the town. In the following century the Clan Ross was to be a Whig Clan, with no sympathy for the Jacobite cause.

A list of grievances was brought against him by his clan: the complaints included his failure to protect his clan in their just and lawful affairs, not keeping courts, not doing justice to the lieges, his absence from burials and public meetings throughout the shire for fear, it was said, of his neighbour George Mackenzie, the Master of Tarbat – but what caused his clansmen particular distress was his interest in practical work 'properly belonging to weemen as their vertue and no ways incumbent for men, whose spirit is farr above these mean things'.

Both he and his wife had a great interest in architecture, and David increased his debts by restoring many churches in the area. He also repaired the Balnagown bridge and was criticized by the clan for lack of propriety when he sat chatting with the workmen. The couple directed much of their efforts to remodelling and extending the castle. Sir George Mackenzie of Tarbat (later First Earl of Cromartie), was engaged on building one of the grandest houses in the area at New Tarbat. The Balnagown Rosses could not lose face.

Some of the building accounts survive. In 1668 the laird was ordering timber work and furniture from Alexander Ross, carpenter of Inverness, including 'all the timber work from the found stone till the rigging stone . . . also scaffolds to the measones [masons] and ane centrie [centring] to the uper vault . . . to compleit . . . wholl work betwix this and . . May 1669 . . . David Ross alwayes furnishing all sort of timber . . requyered [i.e. from the woodland on his estates]'. Payment was to be partly in kind: 'four bolls oat meal, two bolls malt, two stone butter, and sexteine of Cheise . . . betwix this and Junii nixt . . 130 merks . . . betwix this and tenth day of August . . 130 merks qn halfe of the work is done . . . 140 merks on completing the work . .'

It seems to have been at this time that the original rectangular tower-house became an L-shaped building, with a new wing extending from its north-east corner and a turnpike staircase in the angle between the two wings. The fortifications were dismantled and glass was put in the windows, more turrets were added, and the thatched roof replaced by slates. A view of the castle after these alterations can be seen in the background of an early eighteenth-century portrait of a child, which was once at Balnagown.

The initials and coats of arms of David and his wife survive in several places in the castle: in the carved panels which were incorporated into the early nineteenth-century loggia along the west front, on a monogram stone bearing the intertwined letters 'D AS' and the date 1672 beside the present main entrance to the castle, and most spectacularly on the magnificent carved chimney piece at the north end of the Trophy Room, the old laird's hall, which was transformed. The Rosses followed the fashion of the time, adorning the room with paintings and religious texts. Fragments of this decoration were uncovered in the last century.

Some of the correspondence between the couple has survived. The letters from Lady Anne to her husband are affectionate, but forceful. It seems clear that she was the driving force behind these improvements – and, as we shall see, she was not the last châtelaine of Balnagown to leave her mark on the structure of the castle. Whatever her husband's financial straits she was determined that Balnagown should be a splendid residence, as she wrote to him in 1672: 'You must make all things of bewty & ornament & vs [use] . . . & I love to see a house not straited or minsed [with no economies] but it must have aneugh roome in large and nobel manner.'

David Ross was very conscious of his family's great past and pored over old documents in the castle in an attempt to trace his possible claim to Earldom of Ross. He was also aware that he had no heir. Although he had fathered a number of illegitimate children, his marriage remained childless.

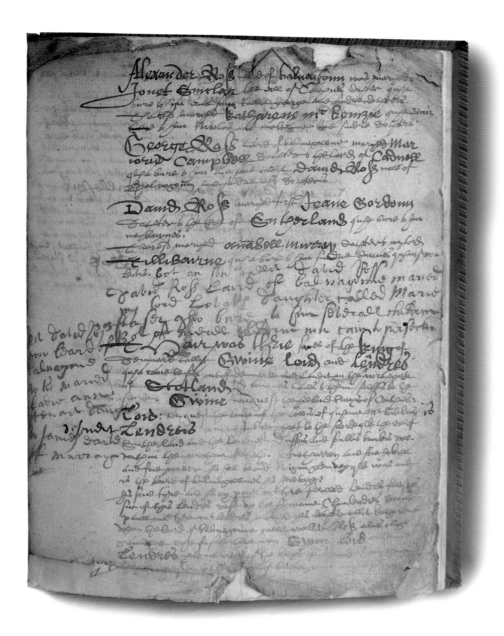

ABOVE: *The 'Breve Cronicle of the Erllis of Ross' includes a short history of the Lairds of Balnagown. It originally ended with the Eleventh Laird, but was brought up to date at the end of the century by his grandson, David Ross, the Thirteenth Laird, whose untidy addition to the text can be seen on this page.*

There were three parties interested in the estates and lands. Lady Anne hoped that her nephew Francis Stewart, a younger son of the Earl of Moray, might take over the estate. In 1685 David Ross had made an agreement with the Earl that in return for a payment of £10,000 the estate would pass to Francis on his death, and Francis was involved in running the Balnagown finances during David's absences. But the Ross clan had no desire for the property to become an appanage of the Earldom of Moray. In any case, as has been seen, a second contender, Lord Ross of Halkhead, already had a considerable financial interest in Balnagown. Finally, the castle could remain the seat of the hereditary Chiefs of the Clan only if the heirs to the chiefdom, the Pitcalnie Rosses, descendants of a younger son of the infamous Alexander, could raise the money needed to redeem the mortgages. This they were unable to do.

David himself seems to have favoured the passing of Balnagown to his Lowland namesakes, the Rosses of Halkhead. In 1706, with the consent of the Laird, Francis Stewart conveyed the estate to Lord Ross, and the heirs male of his body. He did his best to help them in their pursuit of the earldom, forfeiting in their favour any claim he might have to the title. In 1710, the year before his death, David Ross headed the signatories of a letter from the leading men of the clan to Charles Ross, Lord Ross's half-brother who had recently been elected to represent Ross-shire in Parliament. They promised to take 'every opportunity to advance your interest which we now look upon to be the common advantage of all our name & family.'

The Thirteenth Laird of Balnagown died in 1711. The account recording his funeral expenses survives:

William Duk carpenter New Tarbat for coffin &c.	£180
Wm. Kerr painter in Nairne for Scuthins [escutcheons] and Brauches [brooches]	£360
William Strogg chirurgeon in Miltown imbowelling and sheer cloath	£120
Thomas Fraser Inverness baking cookery flour turkis	£126
T. Robertson Inverness Clarett, Brandies and bottles	£386
half hodged of sack	£96
John McKay Inverness spiceries sweetmeats &c.	£256
Murnings [mournings] from Edinburgh	£204
paper, wacks &c. for writting funerall letters	£35
Given out by Jean Stewart one of the servants for murnings	£291

Lady Anne made sure that the last of the old line of Rosses went out in style. His monument in Fearn Abbey proclaims him as 'priscorum Rossiae comitum genuina soboles . . . amplissimae Rossiorum familiae philarchus' ('real offspring of the old Earls of Ross . . . Chief of the great family of the Rosses'). His wife died eight years later, in 1719.

TOP: *The intertwined letters AS and D carved on a plaque set into the exterior wall of the castle stand for Anne Stewart and her husband David Ross, who inherited Balnagown in 1653 when still a child.*

ABOVE: *Baron David Ross, the last of the Ross Lairds of Balnagown of the O'Beolain dynasty, died in 1711. He and his wife were buried at Fearn beneath a monument recording his descent from the Earls of Ross.*

The Eighteenth Century: Newcomers – the Rosses of Halkhead

THE HALKHEAD ROSSES attracted some later historians' disapproval for the manner of their acquisition of Balnagown, and for their pretensions to be Earls of Ross and leaders of the Ross clan, whose coat of arms and crest they adopted instead of their own. The antiquary Charles Fraser-Mackintosh wrote: 'In the annals of Scotland there is, perhaps, no greater case of fraud and wrong than the unscrupulous, but ultimately successful attempts of Lord Ross, and General Charles Ross, strangers to the family, to possess themselves of the estate of Balnagown.'

ABOVE: *A gatepost carved with a hawk's head, the crest of the Rosses of Halkhead, is one of the few reminders of the Lairds of Balnagown in the first half of the eighteenth century.*
LEFT: *The Honourable Charles Ross, Colonel of the 5th Dragoons was the first member of the Lowland family of Ross of Halkhead to be Laird of Balnagown. This portrait by Sir Godfrey Kneller shows him in appropriately martial dress. As a professional soldier he had served under King William III and Marlborough.*

William, Lord Ross had indeed been shrewd and persistent in his pursuit of the estate, but he obtained the property by fair means, and moreover with the approval of most of the Ross Clan. The advent of the Halkhead Rosses was undoubtedly to the advantage of Balnagown. It meant the end of the financial insecurity that had hung over the estate for more than a century.

Lord Ross came close to acquiring the ancient Earldom (a title which would have given him precedence over all the local nobility), but one who stood to lose status was Sir George Mackenzie of Tarbat, Secretary of State for Scotland, who had recently been created Earl of Cromartie. Cromartie wrote dismissively of 'the fidling of this hot-headed fool' who was 'ane old west country laird, knowing nothing of the Earledome of Ross, of the Earles, of their rights, of their rise or fall, and having not more relation to them, directly or indirectly, than the milner of Carstairs has to the Prince of Parma.' His opposition helped put a stop to Lord Ross's ambitions in this direction.

As for their claim to be chiefs of the Clan Ross, there is no doubt that the Halkhead Rosses were widely regarded as such. True, they were not blood relations of the O'Beolain Rosses, but they shared the same name and, what was as important, they had control of the ancestral land of the Ross Chiefs. It was declared in 1712 that all future inheritors of the estate were to use the arms of Ross of Balnagown and adopt Ross as their surname. The claims of the Pitcalnie Rosses, who had been disappointed in their attempt to gain Balnagown, but who still regarded themselves as the true hereditary Chiefs of the Clan, were not officially recognized until 1903. The present Chief is their descendant, David Ross of Shandwick.

It is not known why Lord Ross presented Balnagown to his bachelor half-brother, **Lieutenant-General Charles Ross**, who now became its **Fourteenth Laird**. Perhaps he himself was too deeply involved in political affairs to attend to the estate: he was appointed Lord High Commissioner of the Church of Scotland in 1704 and was one of the sixteen Scottish peers elected to the House of Lords after the Act of Union with England in 1707.

Charles Ross was a professional soldier. Like his brother, he had not at first supported William of Orange and in 1690 had been committed to the Tower for his involvement in Sir James Montgomerie's Jacobite plot. He later served loyally under King William, and then under Marlborough. The descendants of the old Ross chiefs were generally pro-Hanoverian and the Rosses did not join the Jacobite rebellion of 1715. In those anxious times Charles Ross was still seen as a security risk, however. He was one of the officers dismissed from the army and was forced to sell his regiment, the 5th Dragoons.

Balnagown flourished during his lairdship: at last the mortgaged estates could be redeemed and the Laird was able to undertake improvements to the property. He entered enthusiastically into his new Ross-shire inheritance, following his predecessors in serving as Provost of Tain. When he took over Balnagown, he had already been the local MP for two years. One of his parliamentary services was as a member of the secret committee inquiring into the South Sea Company scandal, when he told the House of Commons that he had helped to uncover 'a train of deepest villainy and fraud that hell ever contrived to ruin a nation'.

He died at Bath in 1732 and was buried in Fearn Abbey with a modest memorial extolling in Latin his military virtues. The succession to Balnagown had already been arranged. The estate was to pass to the General's young great-nephew and namesake, **Charles Ross**. He was only eleven when he became the **Fifteenth Laird of Balnagown**, and even before he came of age he was returned in 1741 as MP for Ross-shire. Described as 'a very handsome young man', he followed his great-uncle into a military career. Before he could make any real impression on his Balnagown inheritance the young laird was killed at the Battle of Fontenoy on 30 April 1745. William Collins's 'Ode to a Lady on the Death of Colonel Charles Ross' written to comfort Ross's fiancée, describes the young warrior welcomed in heaven by heroes of the past:

> The warlike dead of every age
> Who fill the fair recording page
>   Shall leave their sainted rest,
> And half-reclining on his spear
> Each wondering chief by turns appear
>   To hail the blooming guest.

When Prince Charles Edward Stuart arrived in Scotland in 1745 to launch his bid to reclaim the throne for the Stuarts, the Ross Clan faced divided loyalties: the Halkhead Rosses and Alexander Ross of Pitcalnie remained anti-Jacobite, but Alexander's son Malcolm joined the rebel army and persuaded many Rosses not to take up arms against the Pretender. In February 1746 the Earl of Loudon, commander of Government forces in Scotland, quartered his army at Balnagown. He had withdrawn from Inverness after a skirmish with the Jacobite army at Moy. This was Bonnie Prince Charlie's last taste of success: a few weeks later he met final defeat nearby on Culloden Moor.

One of the officers in Loudon's army injured in the 'Rout of Moy' was young Charles Ross's elder brother **William, Master of Ross**, who had now become the **Sixteenth Laird of Balnagown**. Lord Ross was now well aware that the family's hold on Balnagown was precarious. He worried about his elder son: 'I own to you freely,' he wrote in a letter in 1746, 'that if my son doe not marry soon and would incline sometimes to live in that country [i.e. Balnagown], I would grudge every expense about Balnagown . . . you know that estate has cost me much . . . and if it was to go out of my family I should be a loser by it . . .'

His fears were realized. On his death in 1754, William became Fourteenth Lord Ross, but he survived his father for only two months. The extinction of the male line of the Halkhead Rosses meant that the succession to Balnagown passed to the family of Sir James Lockhart, the son of General Ross's niece, to whose descendants the General had entailed the estate if such a circumstance arose. In 1756 Lockhart successfully applied to the House of Lords to confirm his right to Balnagown.

RIGHT: *A detail of the 1662 edition of John Speed's map of the Kingdom of Scotland. In the centre Balnagown castle is clearly marked. The land of the Rosses extended west and north-west, adjoining the territory of the Earls of Sutherland.*

John Lockhart Ross: Naval Hero and Agricultural Reformer

ABOVE: *The Baronetcy of Nova Scotia which the William Lockhart of Carstairs had been granted in 1672 was passed down through the Lockhart Rosses of Balnagown. Their badge, now on loan to the Tain Museum, is encircled not, as was usual, by the motto of the order, but by the Ross motto: 'Spem successus alit'.*

OPPOSITE: *The portrait of John Lockhart Ross in the Drawing Room is based on one painted by Sir Joshua Reynolds in 1761. The naval exploits of Captain (later Admiral) Lockhart Ross had made him a national hero by the time he inherited Balnagown.*

THE LOCKHARTS OF CARSTAIRS were an influential family in Lanarkshire, with their seat at Lockhart Hall. William Lockhart had been granted a Baronetcy of Nova Scotia by Charles II in 1672. On having his claim to Balnagown confirmed by the House of Lords and becoming the **Seventeenth Laird**, Sir James, the Fourth Baronet, changed his name to **James Ross-Lockhart**, but he died childless in 1760 before making any impression on his new acquisition. His brother George then inherited the baronetcy, but Balnagown passed to the youngest brother, John.

As the fifth son, Captain John Lockhart – he soon added Ross to his name – had never expected to inherit Balnagown, and when he came into his inheritance at the age of thirty-eight he seized the opportunity to put into order the property which had suffered neglect since the death of his uncle, General Charles Ross. **John Lockhart Ross, the Eighteenth Laird**, was to be one of the most celebrated Lairds of Balnagown.

He had gone to sea at the age of fourteen and had enjoyed a distinguished naval career. Appointed Captain of the *Tartar* in 1756, for two years he had phenomenal success cruising the English Channel in search of French privateers. 'During this period of service . . . he took nine privateers . . . amounting in all to two thousand five hundred prisoners of war, and two hundred and twenty guns, while he had only five men killed and two wounded in the different engagements.' Captain Lockhart had received a hero's welcome on his return, when he was fêted by the merchants of London who presented him with an inscribed cup and salver, and the merchants of Bristol who presented him with a gold cup.

Thus when he came into possession of Balnagown he was already a celebrity. On the strength of his naval success he was returned as Member of Parliament for Linlithgow Burghs in

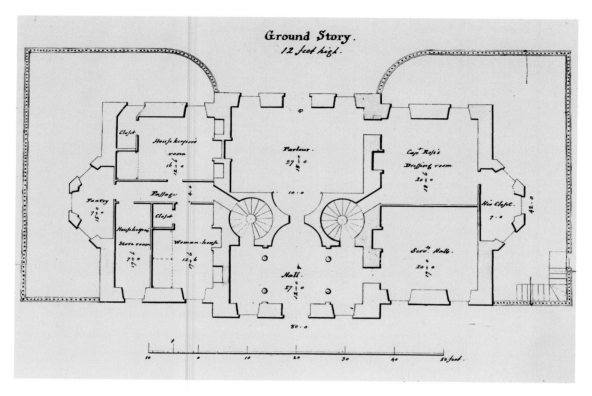

Balnagown as it might have been. In 1762 John Lockhart Ross commissioned the architect John Adam to make preliminary designs for a new Palladian residence to be erected on the bowling green south of the old castle. The castle would have been demolished when the new mansion was built.

1761, and the following year married the wealthy heiress Elizabeth, daughter of Robert Dundas, the Lord President of the Court of Session for Scotland. She inherited from her mother, Henrietta Baillie Carmichael, properties at Lamington and Bonnington in Lanarkshire, which were now added to the Balnagown property. (The connection with Lamington is still recalled today in the name of Lamington Park on the Balnagown estate north of the castle.) It was through Elizabeth's family – descendants of Sir William Wallace – that the famous Wallace Chair once in the Tower of Lamington came to Balnagown.

Captain Lockhart Ross (he inherited the baronetcy from his brother in 1778, and was promoted rear-admiral in 1779) was a man who believed in progress. The revenues from his extensive Lowland properties and the booty he had won in his naval exploits (naval captains were permitted to keep one quarter of what they captured) provided him with funds to invest in his new estate. Navy life had made him appreciate method and discipline, but he was also humane. In the words of a biographer:

> That he was a rigid disciplinarian did not arise from a sternness of character or a love of power, for he was gentle in his nature, and possessed all the mild qualities of humanity; but from a sense of his duty . . . he never failed to combine the manners of gentleman with the feelings of a man.

It was in 1762, after selling the family estate at Lockhart Hall in Lanarkshire, that John Lockhart Ross styled himself 'Ross of Balnagown' and adopted as his own the Ross arms and crest.

Before taking up residence at Balnagown, Captain Lockhart Ross ordered designs for a new house to replace the ancient castle, which at first he intended to demolish. The architect chosen was John Adam, the eldest of the Adam brothers. A new wing at Arniston House, the seat of the Dundas family in Midlothian, had recently been designed by John Adam, so it is likely that the choice of architect for Balnagown came through the Captain's future wife. Adam had already worked for landowners in north-east Scotland, designing, for instance, the dour new façade of Castle Grant for Sir Ludovick Grant of Grant. For Balnagown he produced designs for a new four-storey mansion to be built at the south end of the bowling green at Balnagown.

In the event, the proposed house was not built and the Captain contented himself with remodelling and extending the old castle. In 1763, probably with John Adam as architect, the space between the two wings of the L-shaped building was filled in to provide a house on an almost square plan with projecting south-facing bow. This elegant addition is very different from the earlier parts of the castle. Today the contrast between the still feudal atmosphere of the Trophy Room

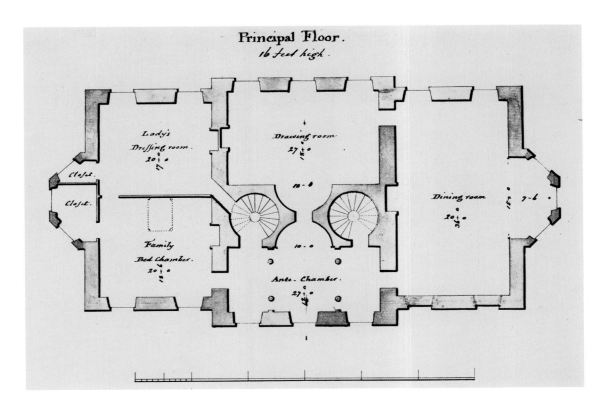

The new house was never built and fortunately the castle survived. Adam's drawings are among the Balnagown papers at the Scottish Record office. One Scottish feature in the otherwise Italianate design is the pair of turnpike (spiral) staircases.

ABOVE: *A portrait of John Adam by Samuel Cotes. Although his designs for a new house at Balnagown were not executed, he was probably responsible for the bow-fronted extension to the castle built in 1763.*

and the more urbane classicism of the light and airy Drawing Room is striking.

Around the castle, new gardens were laid out; 'a road was made in the Castle Green, making 28 days' work at 1/- per day'. The Captain introduced drainage, erected palings to demarcate the policies (i.e. the grounds around the castle), cleared bogs, re-made roads, repaired the bank of the river, planted thousands of young fir trees, and built the large walled kitchen garden.

The castle was no longer the tower-house of a traditional clan chief, but a commodious residence suitable for a modern and forward-looking landlord. In 1765 the new laird moved to Balnagown and from then on made it his principal residence.

Thomas Pennant, the English traveller who toured Scotland in 1768, described John Lockhart

Balnagown in 1780:
an artist's impression

The bow-fronted addition was built for Captain John Lockhart Ross in 1763.

Ross as 'the best farmer and the greatest planter in the country; his wheat and turnips showed the one, his plantation of a million pines the other'. He was a classic example of a new sort of Highland landowner who emerged in the eighteenth century.

By the eighteenth century Highland farming had reached a crisis, as the population rapidly outstripped resources. Easter Ross experienced a series of bad harvests in the 1770s and a serious famine in 1782. Coming as he did from the Lowlands, where modernization of husbandry was already advanced, it is not surprising that John Ross was impatient with the ancient methods of agriculture that he found in the north.

The system of land tenure in the Highland clans was based on pieces of land or 'tacks' let by the Chief, as the principal landowner, to his principal supporters ('tacksmen'). They then sublet them to clansmen. These formed groups of subtenants (or 'cottars'), who held their land by 'runrig', that is, they shared the occupation of the land, which was divided up among them in non-contiguous strips. Thus was created a a farming township, called a 'toun', or in Gaelic a *baile*. There was little security of tenure for the cottars, and the system was open to abuse by the tacksmen, whose position as intermediaries between the chief and his clan gave them an influential and powerful role.

Traditionally the Highlanders valued their leisure more than economic gain. The cottars, living in humble single-storey cottages of rubble stone with turfed roofs, used their combined strip holdings for subsistence farming. Oats were ground into meal at the chief's mill for porridge, and perhaps some potatoes were grown. While their womenfolk toiled in the fields, the men would comfort themselves with pride in their clan, whisky, songs and stories.

Livestock farming grew in importance in the

seventeenth century in the Highlands. It was traditionally based on cattle rearing. 'Black cattle' were the red and gold ancestors of the familiar shaggy Highland breed. They were so called because they were raised on the low-lying 'black' land, free from snow and ice. Unable to survive mountain winters, they were only taken to higher ground for summer grazing. When fattened they were mostly paid as rent to the chief, who arranged for them to be driven south to market. By the end of the seventeenth century a money economy was becoming established: many Highland farmers were paying some of their rents in cash and so were also involved in some trade in livestock on their own account. As an added income, landowners such as Baron David Ross began to exploit the timber resources on their estates.

The following decades saw an acceleration of these changes, as the eighteenth century brought a new approach to landowning. Fundamental attitudes to the land changed: it was no longer seen as a source of manpower and rents, but as a resource to be exploited for productivity and profit. This meant the replacement of the runrig system by larger, more efficient modern farms. In the Highland region it also brought the introduction of large-scale sheep-farming to replace the old inefficient farming of the cottars.

As a naval man, Lockhart Ross had not had much experience of husbandry, but he methodically set about learning to be a farmer. He was in tune with the latest ideas and to prepare for his reforms at Balnagown he consulted the burgeoning host of agricultural text books.

From the start, he recognized the importance of improving communications in the region. In 1764, for instance, he was organizing the building of a new road from Beauly to Dingwall. At the same time, in a steadfast and determined manner he began setting the estates in order and took the land immediately around Balnagown under his own direct control. He appointed an English farm manager, John Baldrey, who was enthusiastic about the prospects. In 1763 he was writing to his employer:

OPPOSITE: *The castle from the southwest. John Lockhart Ross's bow-fronted addition now forms the centre of the south front.*
ABOVE: *Portrait miniature of John Lockhart by Francis Cotes in 1758, painted two years before the gallant Captain inherited Balnagown and adopted the name Ross.*

TOP: *A Cheviot sheep: the introduction of this breed to the region by John Lockhart Ross and by other proprietors meant the end of the old Highland way of life.*
ABOVE AND RIGHT: *Much of the land around Balnagown is used for sheep and arable farming, as it was in John Lockhart Ross's day.*

I consider not to have oxen ploughing any longer, 4 able horses will do twice the business . . . to have 200 stots this year and as many sheep . . . to sow about 20 acres turnips among the barley, oats & wheat . . . to sow plenty clover & trefoil in order to keep them from turnips until Christmas . . . to sow some tetches, will introduce black oats and fetches for horse seed, save the white oats for meal, sow some carrots & give the horses some straw, chaff and horsebeans. Some land that is very fallow – sow rape and it will get it clean. All men will be by the year which will make great differences than by the day. I am persuaded I can grow hops here.

Lockhart Ross had no time for the old runrig system and wanted the cottars each to have their own holdings. In a letter of 1777 he declared that it would be to the 'great service of the tenants' if 'every man's farm is set apart and not run rig as they usually are', and asked his grieve (farm bailiff) to 'put such a value on each man's farm as you think they can pay . . . with judgment and impartial justice between me and the tenants.'

In 1777 he had returned for a time to active service at the outbreak of war with France, but he still kept a close eye on his estates and an enthusiasm for their improvement, even when at sea. In a letter to his grieve on 2 November he wrote:

Dear MacCulloch,
We have completed 9 weeks exercise and had not the good fortune to fall in with the French fleet, but took nine of the French merchant ships valued at about £10,000. . . you will dispose of the salmon to the best advantage, and let me know what they made and what they sold at, and the whole of the butter, cheese, calves and lambs and pray take good care of the foles of the Spanish mare, as I wish to raise a good breed of Highland horses.

The Admiral has an ambivalent reputation in Highland history. He is remembered as a benevolent landlord but also as a reformer whose innovations helped bring about the destruction of the old Highland way of life. He was notably generous to his tenantry in the terrible famine of 1782-83. In the *Statistical Account* of 1792 the local minister described the laird's reaction to the disaster:

Sir John, with a liberality which does him the highest credit, understanding the lamentable situation of the poor people, sent to be distributed to the sufferers on his own estates a seasonable and bountiful supply of pease, barley, flour and potatoes; to which noble beneficence many hundreds owed their lives. He also ordered his factor to give his Highland tenants in Kincardine who did not save as much as would sow their crofts, seed from his farms in the low country, where the failure was not nearly so great as in the high grounds and straths, and upon his return home at the conclusion of the war, he discounted one-third of the arrears of rent over the whole of his estates.

Yet as one of the first to introduce Lowland sheep to the Highlands, he is seen as an initiator of the Highland Clearances which left much of northern Scotland bereft of its human inhabitants.

The traditional Highland sheep – small, scrawny animals – had not been central to the farming economy. They provided only milk, wool and meat for the poor cottars. Lockhart Ross recognized that this was not making the most of the resources and in 1778, during his wartime naval service, he set his mind to the improvement of sheep-farming.

Passing through Perthshire he had seen flocks of black-faced Linton sheep and was told they could produce three times as much meat as cattle kept on the same acreage of ground. Many southern sheepfarmers believed that their breeds would not survive further north. Lockhart Ross was not convinced by their doubts. He took one large farm near Balnagown under his immediate control and successfully introduced a flock of Lintons. He then granted the lease to one Thomas Geddes, the first Lowland sheepfarmer to come north.

Geddes showed that the coastal lands of Ross-shire were well-suited for this type of sheep, but that a hardier breed would be even more profitable, and would thrive better on the harsher uplands. The Cheviot sheep fitted the

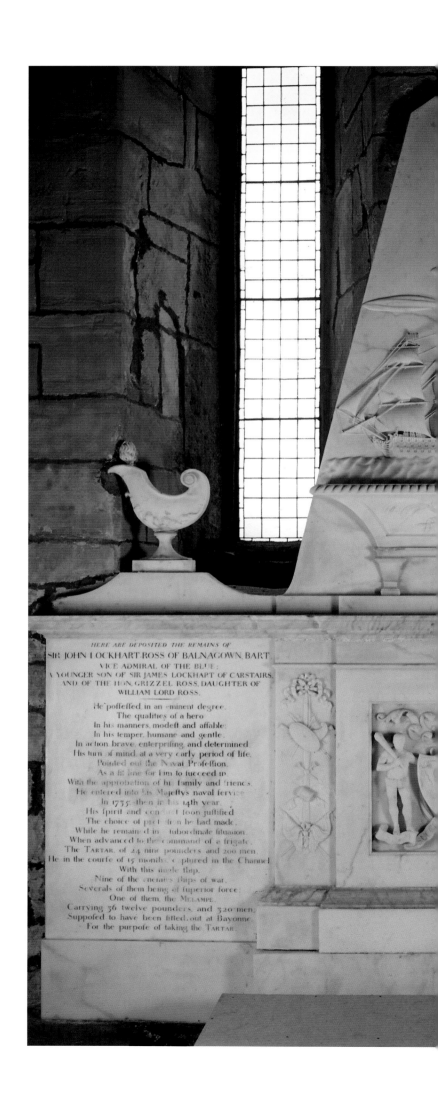

purpose admirably and has remained the breed in the region ever since. It was adopted in Caithness by another agricultural improver, Sir John Sinclair, with equal success.

The local farmers realized that this new sheep economy would inevitably spell the end of their traditional livelihood. As Sir George Mackenzie recalled in his account of agricultural progress in the region, 'the most wicked and flagrant depredations were committed on Mr Geddes' stock; numbers were shot, and droves were collected, surrounded, and forced in lakes and drowned.' Nevertheless, Sinclair and Lockhart Ross persisted. Both believed that their improvements could be brought in gradually with due consideration for their tenants. Lockhart Ross was strongly opposed to the emigration of the Highlanders. He had plans to establish cloth mills at Kincardine to create new employment, but these came to nothing.

The Highland cottars continued to resist change, and in 1792, the 'Year of the Sheep', when large-scale clearances began in Easter Ross, including the Balnagown estates, the people rose in revolt. After the collapse of this uprising nothing stood in the way of the introduction of sheep. The Highland Clearances caused great distress, but most of the thousands of Highlanders who left their land to emigrate overseas stood a chance at least of becoming more prosperous and healthier than they had been under the oppressive old clan system, where they were often living on the edge of starvation.

Admiral Sir John Lockhart Ross died in 1790 and was buried in the Ross vault at Fearn Abbey. His grandiose monument, incorporating the Ross coat of arms, with the badge of a Baronet of Nova Scotia and a carving of the *Tartar*, has a lengthy inscription paying eloquent tribute to his achievements.

LEFT: *Sir John Lockhart Ross has the grandest of the Ross monuments in Fearn Abbey. His activities on land and sea are commemorated in words and images.*

The Nineteenth Century: Balnagown Transformed

FOUR OF THE FIVE SONS of Sir John Lockhart Ross and Lady Elizabeth followed distinguished careers in the army or navy, while their third son George followed in the steps of his maternal grandfather, entering the legal profession and later becoming a judge. The heir to the estate and to the baronetcy was the eldest son, **Sir Charles Ross**, a major in the 37th Regiment of Foot, who in 1790 became Balnagown's **Nineteenth Laird**.

In 1800 he was appointed colonel of the 85th Foot, and six years later was entrusted with raising a new regiment, the 86th, in Ireland, equipping and training the soldiers for service in the European wars. A letter from one of his recruiting officers gives a flavour of this work:

> Sir, I have a very successful response over the last week in the Kilkenny district. I have to report 120 men of reasonable condition for the new foot regiment . . . the men are signed and paid 1/- . . . They should be ready for shipping to the Peninsula in one month.

ABOVE: *Count James Lockhart-Wishart, the father of Sir Charles Ross's first wife, was an officer in the Imperial armies. His dashing portrait in Austrian uniform hangs at Balnagown on the main staircase. The statue of a girl on the left, by the Florentine sculptor Bazzanti, is one of the many nineteenth-century carrara marble statues which decorate the castle.*

LEFT: *Officer and Private of the 85th Regiment of Foot in late-eighteenth century uniforms. Sir Charles Ross commanded the regiment in the Napoleonic Wars.*

OPPOSITE: *Sir Charles Ross (1763-1814), Seventh Baronet and Nineteenth Laird of Balnagown, painted by Sir John Watson Gordon. Like his predecessors as Lairds of Balnagown, he made his career in the services, he also took a close interest in the estates and was active in local politics. His portrait hangs in the Gallery in the Castle's east wing.*

At Balnagown he continued his father's scientific husbandry of the estates, which by this time covered nearly half a million acres, mainly in Ross-shire, but extending into Sutherland. Although he was a professional soldier, he was also active in public affairs. Like his father he was a Member of Parliament, representing Tain Burghs and later Ross-shire, and he also found time to serve as Provost of Tain.

By his first marriage, to his cousin Matilda-Theresa Lockhart-Wishart, a celebrated beauty and – thanks to an honour bestowed on her father, who had fought in the Imperial armies on the Continent – a Countess of the Holy Roman Empire, he had two children. The son died young, and the descendants of the daughter, Matilda, eventually inherited her grandmother's estates.

Matilda-Theresa died in 1791, and in 1799 Sir Charles married again. He had met his second wife during his military service in Ireland. Lady Mary Fitzgerald, as eldest daughter of the Second Duke of Leinster, was a member of the leading family of the Irish aristocracy. Their marriage contract, a formidable document covering many leaves of parchment, was designed to meet the financial consequences of all contingencies. It is now displayed in the Trophy Room.

Lady Mary left her stamp on Balnagown Castle during her more than forty years as châtelaine. Strong-willed, a good businesswoman and a valuable helpmate to her husband, Lady Mary was in some ways reminiscent of her seventeenth-century predecessor, Lady Anne. The two women are remembered in the names given to viewpoints on the estate near the castle: 'Lady Mary's Seat' and 'Lady Anne's Seat'.

In the early nineteenth century poverty was still rife in the Highlands. The surviving rent books from this period show that tenants were given consideration and that their payments of grain in lieu of rent were waived if their circumstances were critical. The Admiral's tradition of dispensing new seed in a bad season was continued. However, such measures could do little to alleviate the general economic misery of the Highlanders at this time, and the drift away to the Lowlands or emigration overseas continued. Insanitary living conditions and overcrowding exacerbated the devastating cholera epidemic which wiped out several families around Balnagown during the hot summer of 1832.

The social welfare of the tenantry was an important concern of Lady Mary: she started the first girls' school on the estate, paying the teacher's salary herself, as well as providing clothes for the girls to enable them to attend, together with books and other expenses. The school remained in operation until 1872.

On her husband's death in 1814 their only surviving son was still only two years old. Lady Mary ably took over the running of the estates, assisted by her Fitzgerald brothers. The extensive lands were kept in good order, but her principal interests were her home, the houses and gardens, and her family, a son and his five sisters. She enjoyed dispensing hospitality at Balnagown and at the other Lockhart Ross seat, Bonnington House in Lanarkshire.

This was an age when many Scottish castles were being enlarged and made more romantic. Lady Mary was a great builder, remodelling and extending the castle and laying out new gardens. Her taste in architecture was very different from that of her father-in-law, the Admiral. Instead of his plain classicism, she preferred the evocative medievalism of the Gothic Revival, the style that had been made popular in Scotland above all by Sir Walter Scott. (In the 1830s Balnagown had a direct link with the memory of Scott; after the novelist's death in 1832, his close friend and amanuensis, William Laidlaw, became the factor.) All Lady Mary's alterations to the castle were in the Gothic manner, and her improvements to the garden were also Romantic: winding paths along the river made the most of the picturesque setting.

Between 1818 and 1821 a Gothic loggia and conservatory were built around the western end of the castle. These were followed by the addition of a Gothic portico

OPPOSITE: *Lady Mary Ross, for forty-three years mistress of Balnagown, looks out benignly from her portrait in the Dining Room. It was painted in the 1830s by the brilliant young artist Andrew Somerville. Lady Mary remodelled the castle and extended it in the Gothic manner to create the striking east wing.*

DUNROBIN CASTLE FROM GARDENS

TOP: *A portrait by Andrew Somerville of Sir Charles Ross (1812-1883), Eighth Baronet and Twentieth Laird, as a young man in the 1830s. A reclusive character and keen sportsman, he played little part in public life and became increasingly eccentric after the death of his first wife. He was nicknamed 'the Jackdaw' and attempts were made to have him certified as insane.*

ABOVE: *Lady Mary Ross may have taken her cue for her alterations at Balnagown from nearby Dunrobin Castle, which was transformed by the Duchess-Countess of Sutherland in the 1830s.*

OPPOSITE: *The view of Lady Mary's east wing from the lawn by the Balnagown River. The terracing of the slope was part of the Italian Garden created here in the 1840s.*

built on the south side between 1832 and 1835, and over the following years a whole new castellated Gothic wing was constructed at the eastern end overlooking the Balnagown River. The ashlar masonry is the pinkish limestone local to Easter Ross. Windows were also opened up on the north side to take advantage of the views along the valley.

Visiting the castle around 1840, Catherine Sinclair, a member of an old Caithness family, was struck by the contrast between old and new:

> The finest residence in this neighbourhood is not in the habit of being shown, but we got a glimpse of Balnagown, belonging to Sir Charles Ross, with a modern addition à la Gillespie, not yet finished inside, but the abbey-like appearance of which is a curious contrast with the old Scotch castle, looking as if it had once belonged to the army, and had now taken orders.

While it is true that the style of this wing is reminiscent of the architect Sir James Gillespie Graham, one of Scotland's leading exponents of the early Gothic Revival, there is no evidence that he designed any of the additions to Balnagown. We do know, however, that in 1818 he designed the new church at Logie Easter not far from the castle and worked for Lady Mary elsewhere, building a new porch at Bonnington House in 1830. There are certain oddities in the planning of the Balnagown wing – the irregular alignment of the doorways in the Gallery, for instance – which suggest that a professional architect was not employed. While the inspiration may well have come from Gillespie Graham, the design itself is probably the work of a gifted amateur, no doubt Lady Mary herself, working with a local builder.

There is a parallel here with building work undertaken a few years earlier at Dunrobin Castle, the seat of the Sutherlands north of the Dornoch Firth. The Duchess-Countess of Sutherland also dispensed with the services of an architect for the Gothic additions she made to the castle between 1835 and 1837. At Dunrobin, too, a new terraced garden was laid out in the 1840s. It is hard not to believe that Lady Mary was emulating on a smaller scale the architectural projects of her northern neighbours.

The interiors of her new wing, and of the library and music room which were remodelled at this time, were decorated with Gothic vaulting and tracery, with exquisite details carved in wood or moulded in plaster, clearly the work of skilled craftsmen. The most attractive of these rooms is perhaps the Gallery with its intricate rib-vaulting and niches, while the Dining Room with magnificent fan-vaulting and a pendant boss, is one of the finest Gothic Revival interiors in Scotland.

The building accounts which survive from this period mention the names of some of the craftsmen involved: the mason was Alexander Ross, the carpenter John Munro, and the plasterer Robert Ross. The appearance twice of the name Ross may indicate that these were local men.

Large sums were spent on elegant furniture, fabrics and fittings. Lady Mary had 'the handsomest curtains ordered from London, cabinetmakers in Edinburgh making richly carved antique furniture, new leather cues for the billiard room, etc.'

For her improvements to the castle policies (grounds) Lady Mary sought expert advice. To lay out her garden by the river she employed the head gardener from the Royal Palace of Holyrood in Edinburgh.

It is a remarkable fact that from 1814 to 1942 the lairdship of Balnagown passed through only two generations, since the last two Ross lairds both inherited the estate as minors. By the time Lady Mary died in 1842, her son **Sir Charles Ross, the Twentieth Laird** and Eighth Baronet, was already thirty years of age. He had received a good education at Eton and Christ Church, Oxford, but because of his weakness of character and eccentric behaviour he had not been given responsibilities; his mother had continued to run the estates until her death. Significantly, even after the baronet came of age in 1833 it was his mother's coat of arms that was placed over the entrance to the castle.

In 1833 Sir Charles was faced with an important decision. His grandmother, Lady Baillie-Ross, Admiral Ross's widow, had died in 1817, leaving her estates of Lamington in trust until her grandson attained his majority and chose either Lamington or Balnagown as his seat. His choice fell on Balnagown, and consequently

ABOVE: *The craftsmanship of the decorative details in the new wing was of the highest quality. This is a corner of the Dining Room.*

LEFT: *This view from the south-east shows the 'abbey-like appearance' of the new addition to Balnagown which Catherine Sinclair noted in 1840. The building in the foreground is thought to have been the entrance to the ice-house.*

Lamington passed to the son of his half-sister Matilda, who had married Admiral Sir Thomas Cochrane. The Wallace Chair, however, came to Balnagown.

Sir Charles was a strange man. He took little interest in the management of his property, and was reluctant to mix with his fellow landowners. His behaviour became more erratic after the death in 1848 of his first wife, his cousin, Elizabeth Lockhart Ross, whom he had married in 1841. During her years at the castle she had created the Italian Gardens below the castle along the Balnagown River, which were completed shortly before her death. Their marriage had been childless.

Various stories are told about the eccentric laird. During dinner he would go into a corner of the dining room and stand on his head. He enjoyed playing pranks. Often he would retreat up an oak tree in the castle grounds and have his food taken out to him there, earning him the nickname 'the Jackdaw' (a name later adopted by a hotel at nearby Barbaraville). Attempts were made to have him committed as being of unsound mind, but they were unsuccessful. He was painfully aware of his mental problems, as his gamekeeper, Thomas Robertson, recalled: 'He often talked about his feelings to me. He always said he was so nervous, and that he knew there was a screw loose. He said so often, but he could not tell what it was.'

There was some improvement in his condition when, having remained a widower for seventeen years, he married again at the age of fifty-three, at a midnight ceremony on 2 March 1865. His second wife, Rebecca Sophia, the daughter of a certain Henry Barnes of Tufnell Park in London, was able to control her husband's more bizarre behaviour and take some of the responsibility for looking after the estates.

The later nineteenth century was the golden age of sport in the Highlands. Now that the region was largely depopulated, it had acquired the aura of a romantic wilderness and its potential as a playground for the rich was first realized. The romance of deerstalking was spread by such writers as Charles St John who in 1833 stalked the celebrated 'muckle hart of Benmore' on the Balnagown estates — 'easily the most famous stag

ABOVE: *Deerstalking became a popular sport in the nineteenth century. The newly-built Deanich Lodge in one of the finest deer forests in the Balnagown estates was photographed towards the end of the century with the keeper and his family.*
RIGHT: *Fishing today on the Balngown estate near the castle.*

ever shot in Scotland'. Impetus was given to the sport by Prince Albert at Balmoral, and by the popularity of Sir Edwin Landseer's evocative paintings, and in the latter part of the century deerstalking had become a fashionable activity for anyone who could afford it. Railways made access to the north of Scotland much easier than it had been; Balnagown itself was now only a short distance from the main line north to Caithness.

So sheep-grazing gave way to deer forests on many estates. On the heather moorlands grouse-shooting took over, and many people discovered the pleasures of salmon fishing. Benmore, Strathoykel, Braelangwell and other parts of the Balnagown estates were well suited to these activities, and as on many Highland estates, stalking, shooting and fishing now took pride of place. Sport remains an important part of the Balnagown estates today.

Although the eccentric Sir Charles's reclusive habits meant that he played little part in the social gatherings usually associated with sport in the Highlands at this time, shooting and fishing were his principal passion. He was an excellent shot and spent as much time as possible out on the hill.

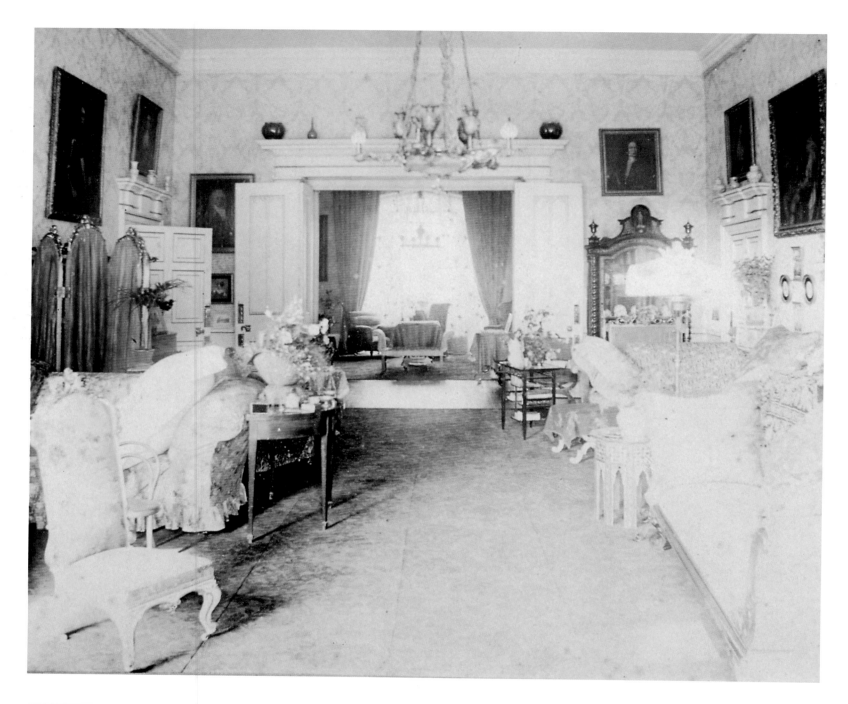

ABOVE: *The Drawing Room photographed towards the end of the nineteenth century. Note the arrangement of the furniture typical of the time with sofas and tables lining the room. (Compare the photograph on pages 128-129.)*

LEFT: *The bedroom in the east wing photographed in the late nineteenth century. The Ross arms appear on the headboard. (See also the photograph on page 137).*

OPPOSITE: *Rebecca Barnes became Lady Ross in March 1865, when she married the eccentric baronet at a secret midnight ceremony. This photograph was taken around the turn of the century.*

In an obituary of her husband his widow wrote
with some warmth: 'He always appeared
delighted at the approach of the shooting season
when his period of migration to the hills he loved
so well came round. Sir Charles was well-known
for his kindness of heart and attachment to his
tenants and dependants.'

In 1872, at the age of fifty-eight, he had at last
produced an heir. As a prank, he had promptly
hidden the baby in the castle and made the
servants search for it. When he died in 1883 and
was buried in the new family vault in Kincardine
churchyard (the monument can be seen from the
road that runs past the church), his son was only
eleven years old. Like his father before him, the
young **Sir Charles Henry Augustus Frederick
Ross, Balnagown's Twenty-first Laird,** spent
his early years with his mother managing the
estate for him. For this she received little thanks.

Rebecca was another of the remarkable women
who have guided the destinies of Balnagown. A
cosmopolitan woman with many interests, she
was an accomplished author who published
several verse dramas under the name 'R.S. Ross',
as well as a couple of closely argued pamphlets
attacking Prime Minister Gladstone's handling of
the Eastern Question. She kept an eye on the management of Balnagown, with the advice of Colonel
Robert Ross, the father of her husband's first wife.
But her time was divided between Balnagown,
Bonnington and London, and she was often
abroad with her relatives and friends in Paris. This
meant that she could not give the close attention to
estate management that was necessary and much
was left in the hands of her factor and advisors.

In the years since Lady Mary's death the
estates had been managed inefficiently and were
in need of improvement. As late as the 1870s the
cottars' houses on the Balnagown estates were
still being built in a primitive manner, with clay
mortar and turf roofs, at a time when most other
landowners were already constructing more
substantial houses for their tenantry. Rents were
badly in arrears and money had been spent only
on the shooting lodges required for sporting
parties. One lawyer who looked into the affairs
of Balnagown was struck by the inefficiency: 'I
know not why so large an estate should render

so little money.'

Rebecca is remembered, probably unfairly, for
her extravagance. When her son took legal action
against her for dissipating the income of the estate,
any evidence of her profligacy was collected from
the staff: 'There were trips for scarlett cloth, silver
buttons, bleu and lemon taffatie, ribbans, perel
necklaces, gounes and petticoats, gold buckles
and cravats, velvet caps, silk negligees, gold for
louping and tressing hair, etc.'

While the estates were allowed to languish,
she made improvements to the castle itself,
particularly to its gardens. The banks of the river
were planted with bushes and shrubs, and
peaches were grown in a lean-to greenhouse in
the walled garden.

Above all, she lavished money and attention
on her son, who grew up to become perhaps the
most remarkable of all the lairds of Balnagown.

The Last Ross Laird: Writs and Rifles

ABOVE: *Rebecca doted on her only son, Charles, but when he came of age in 1893 he accused her of misappropriating money from the estates during his minority.*
OPPOSITE: *Sir Charles Ross, Ninth Baronet and Twenty-first Laird of Balnagown. This portrait by Charles Hardie was painted in 1894 when the laird came of age. Clad in Hunting Ross tartan, he is dressed as the Clan Chief, with three eagle feathers in his bonnet.*

SIR CHARLES ROSS, TWENTY-FIRST LAIRD OF BALNAGOWN, and Ninth Baronet, was a man of extraordinary vigour and inventive genius, but arrogance, egotism and vindictiveness dissipated much of his energy.

As a young man he had been spoiled and kept from the realities of life. At the age of eighteen he possessed two yachts, a coach-and-four and an unlimited expense account. He had been a success at Eton and at Cambridge, where he had the distinction of being the first married member of the University rowing eight. (He married, against his mother's wishes, shortly after his twenty-first birthday in 1893.) He had been introduced into the best circles of London Society. He returned to Balnagown assuming that he was a rich laird, only to discover that in fact he had little ready money and was well on the way to bankruptcy. On hearing of the outstanding debts and uncollected rents and the lack of investment in the estate, his response was one that would set the pattern for his future behaviour. He began a hectic series of improvements to the estate, issuing orders in a torrent of numbered memos, and he sued his mother, Rebecca, now the Dowager Lady Ross, for funds which he claimed she had taken out of the estate. She had, he alleged, taken advantage of her husband's weakness and death to rob Balnagown. The fact that the greater part of this money had actually been lavished on her son seemed not to weigh with the young baronet. This was when the stories of Rebecca's extravagance were first aired, and there was much unseemly wrangling about furniture, pictures and heirlooms.

Sir Charles's vindictiveness towards his doting mother was extreme; he found the presence of the dowager in the castle unbearable. Matters reached a crisis when he locked her in her room for three weeks. On her release he crept up behind her as she walked along a corridor and with a candle set her long red tresses on fire. She left soon afterwards to live at nearby Scotsburn.

TOP: *Sir Charles Ross had shown precocious talent during his schooldays at Eton, where he began his research into rifle design. As well as being an excellent shot, he was also a fine oarsman, rowing in the Cambridge crew in the 1893 University Boat Race.*

ABOVE: *The Ross Rifle, designed by Sir Charles, was adopted by the Canadian Government before the First World War. He set up an arms factory in Quebec. However, the rifle's delicate mechanism intended for competitive shooting was unsuited to wartime conditions: it jammed in rapid fire and was susceptible to dust and mud.*

His next scandalous encounter in the law courts was with his wife, Winifred (née Berens), whom he had practically abandoned after only two years of marriage. They were divorced in 1897. Winifred had borne him a son, but the sickly child had died at the age of one from tuberculosis, the result, it was said, of having been fed milk from a certain Jersey cow at his father's insistence, against the specific advice of a vet.

Over the following decades the list of those who felt the force of Sir Charles's litigious temper grew steadily: his factors, the Inland Revenue, neighbouring lairds, banks, shopkeepers, the United States government, the Canadian government, the press, lawyers – even personal friends. No wonder that in 1932 the celebrated barrister Sir Norman Birkett KC could write to his friend: 'Dear Charles, Now that the deer stalking season is over, the litigation season commences. What have you for me?'

Sir Charles's ingenuity was not confined to

legal battles, however. He also had a great
aptitude in mechanical matters. At Balnagown
he built a new mill-race and workshop across the
river beside the laundry, for his experiments in
the manufacture of agricultural implements and
rifle making. The library at the castle still contains
many of the technical works he collected.

Rifles were his first and greatest interest.
Like his father before him, he was a fine shot,
and his inquiring mind had been grappling with
the means of improving the design of rifles since
he had been at Eton. While still a schoolboy he
had patented his first rifle, and as an
undergraduate he designed an improved
version which went into production and became
well respected by sportsmen looking for a light
high-velocity rifle. At Balnagown, once he had
set the farming in order, he turned to rifles
again, working closely with his blacksmith. The
result was the Ross Rifle, a firearm with a breech
bolt action, which is still admired as one of the
most accurate rifles ever invented. It won more
prizes at the annual shooting competition at
Bisley than any other rifle before or since. Sir
Charles went to the Boer War equipping the
Ross Machine Gun Battery with guns designed
by himself. He acquitted himself well, but on his
return could not resist suing the British
Government for expenses he had incurred
'helping to win the war'.

The government showed no interest in the
production of the Ross Rifle, but in Canada he
found a more favourable response. The Ross
Rifle Company was founded in Quebec in 1910
and a factory was established there to produce a
version of the rifle for military use. However,
disaster was soon to follow. In the First World
War the Canadian forces arrived in France

TOP: *Winifred Berens became Sir Charles's first wife in 1893.*
The young laird married her, against his mother's wishes, as soon
as he came of age. They were divorced four years later.
RIGHT: *Patricia Ellison from Louisville, Kentucky, married Sir*
Charles in 1901. She lived at Balnagown for only a short time
before moving to London for the sake of her health. She endured
her husband's outrageous behaviour and infidelities before the
couple were finally divorced in 1930.

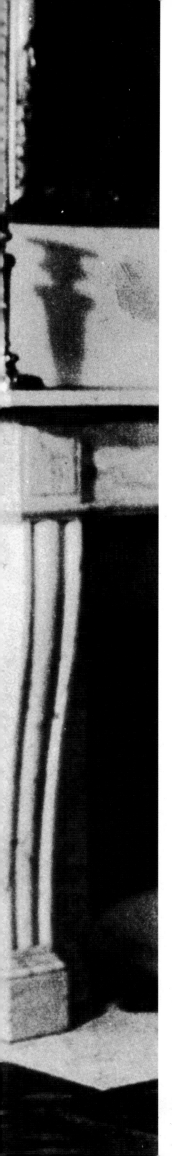

ABOVE: *Sir Charles Ross (far left) at a dinner party in Montreal in February 1899. The laird's business interests often took him across the Atlantic. He established a firearms factory in Quebec in 1910.*

armed with Ross Rifles. But the finely tuned mechanism could not cope with conditions on the Western Front:

> Though satisfactory when used for slow fire, the empty case became jammed in the chamber directly rapid fire began. . . . After about five rounds had been fired it was impossible to work the bolt.

Canadian soldiers threw their weapons away in disgust and rearmed themselves with rifles from the British dead.

This débâcle effectively ended Sir Charles's career as an arms manufacturer, but he was not left out of pocket. When his Quebec factory was acquired by the Canadian government, he had already made around a million pounds. He used this to set up a trust for his second wife, Patricia Ellison, an American beauty from Louisville, whom he had married in 1901.

Lady Patricia had come to Balnagown and tried to play her part as the laird's wife. She was instrumental in setting up the first district nursing service for the area. However, her doctor advised her that the climate in Easter Ross aggravated her asthma and recommended that she live further south. She moved to London.

She soon discovered that marital fidelity was not in Sir Charles's nature. He was cited as co-respondent in innumerable divorce proceedings, and over the following decades he made frequent hunting expeditions in Russia and India and many jaunts to hideaway fishing lodges with a string of female companions. When Patricia eventually began a divorce suit, he retaliated by instituting divorce proceedings against her in the United States. A protracted and acrimonious legal battle of course ensued until the marriage was finally dissolved in 1930.

LEFT: *Dorothy Mercado, Sir Charles's secretary, finally became his third and last wife in 1939. She inherited Balnagown on his death.*

In the meantime Sir Charles had had to confront other problems. The Inland Revenue

ABOVE: *As soon as he attained his majority, Sir Charles threw himself into improving the estates. He brought in new agricultural equipment and set up a workshop by the castle for his own inventions. The photograph taken in 1924 shows him testing a ditching plough on Benmore.*

demanded a share of the fortune he had acquired from his rifle factory and sent him a bill for £360,000, threatening to confiscate Balnagown if it was not paid. This did not daunt the baronet, however, whose response was typically ingenious: he had Balnagown declared a ward of the Delaware Court, making the whole of the lands of Balnagown in effect American territory. He ordered the stars and stripes to be flown from the castle battlements. Any move by the British authorities would be an act of war. Nonplussed by this manoeuvre, the authorities responded in a manner reminiscent of the treatment meted out to Sir Charles's sixteenth-century predecessors, declaring the Laird of Balnagown an outlaw. He was the last British subject to be outlawed. This meant that he could not set foot on British soil without fear of immediate imprisonment.

Thus the result of his cunning victory over the Inland Revenue was exile. He was forced to set up home in the United States and run the estates from there with the dedicated help of his secretary, Dorothy Mercado, who became his third wife in 1939.

Like his great-grandfather, the Admiral, Ross was determined to modernize the farming of his

estates. He was exasperated by the backwardness of the Scots: 'It will probably take Scotland a hundred years to educate itself up to my level,' he once wrote. Many of the improvements he instituted were ahead of their time and have since become common practice. In 1923 a small fortune was spent on bringing caterpillar tractors and combine harvesters across the Atlantic. In 1925 the order was given to build a concrete silo, and a silage harvester was imported.

The cables, letters and carefully numbered memos that poured across the Atlantic were filled with Sir Charles's hectoring impatience and mordant wit:

TO A FACTOR: 'I have come to the conclusion that you are the High Priest of loafers. You have ignored my instruction W896 and disregarded W894. At the moment I am trying to put the United States of America on its feet. Hells Bells, this is a big enough task, and I cannot afford to be distracted by a loafer like you who either cannot read, or is suffering from an alcoholic overdose.'

TO A LONDON BARRISTER: 'Because I was at Eton and your father was at Eton with me, I gave you a brief. Dear boy, you have made a fool, not only of me, but of your father. You will kindly pass the brief to J. Smithers Esq. who, sad to say, was at Harrow, but can only be an improvement.'

TO A FARM MANAGER: 'I employ Miss Chadwick as my financial secretary. You are going into her office and fuddling her brain about manure for Garty Farm. I telephone her from New York to talk about finance. What happens? Her head is cluttered with dung and I get no sense out of her. Keep your dung to yourself or I will come over and rub your damn nose in it.'

He was able to pay occasional clandestine visits to Balnagown, his arrival heralded by firing a gun in the air. But this only heightened his homesickness.

Thriving on activity, he threw himself into a variety of ventures: he bought a game reserve in Tanganyika (where he also planned to open a factory canning wild dog meat for the American market), built electric power stations in North America, manufactured propellers, designed yachts and published an anti-

ABOVE: *Sir Charles on safari. His passion for hunting big game took him to Africa, where he acquired a game reserve in Tanganyika. A lion's head now adorns the Trophy Room.* LEFT: *Sir Charles Ross on the castle steps in the 1920s: at Balnagown he lived 'in the traditional chieftain style, wearing the Highland dress, which his handsome figure can carry so well'.*

Communist newspaper, *The Outlook*.

The Second World War brought a last sparring match with the British Government. Discovering that soldiers were being billeted at Balnagown without his consent, he wrote a sharp letter to Leslie Hore-Belisha, the Minister for War :

Sir – It has come to my notice that British troops have occupied Balnagown Castle in the North of Scotland. You should be aware that Balnagown Castle, which belongs to me, is a ward of the American Courts and this action by British Troops constitutes an occupation of American Territory.

This raises a delicate situation when the British Government are seeking so much sympathy from the USA. Before taking the matter up with the State Department in Washington, I would await your assurance that these foreign troops will be withdrawn forthwith and in future proper respect is shown to USA territories by your Ministry.

ROSS OF BALNAGOWN

The Minister did not reply, but the troops were withdrawn.

The last Ross of Balnagown died in Florida in 1942. He had suffered from a heart condition for some years, but when his doctor had ordered him to rest, his first reaction had been to organize another African safari. During his final illness he still kept up his defiance: when the doctor came to visit him on his sickbed in Florida, the dying laird gasped 'Get the hell out of here.'

His ashes were returned to Scotland where his widow arranged for them to be scattered on the top of Ben More on the Balnagown estate. She sat at the bottom of the mountain with a telescope to make sure the bearers went all the way to the top. When they arrived they found the box containing the casket was fastened with Allen screws. They had no key, so it had to be smashed open on the rocks.

Sir Charles Ross was a difficult and complex character. Yet to the end he always retained the respect and affection of the tenants on the Balnagown estates. Although absent for much of the time, he had been an effective and considerate landlord and by outwitting the law he had held the estates intact. After his death, the future was not going to be easy.

Sir Charles left no legitimate children and his death brought new financial pressures. His widow, who now inherited the castle and estates, faced a difficult task as she tried to preserve the castle and manage the estate. Her husband had set up a complicated structure of corporations and trusts in America to keep the Balnagown estate beyond reach of the taxman, but the laird's cat-and-mouse game that had held the Inland Revenue at bay for years was now over. When the day of reckoning came, Dorothy was forced to sell off thousands of acres of land, including sporting lodges, salmon rivers, hotels and a distillery. Without her husband's brilliant business acumen and devious ingenuity, she found that the estate was dwindling fast.

In 1953 she married again. Together with her new husband, Francis Eveleigh de Moleyns, the younger son of an Irish peer, she attempted to run what was left of the estate as a sporting venture, but without much success. The land was still heavily encumbered with debt – legal fees alone were due for £40,000. By the time Lady Ross died in

ABOVE: *Lady Ross's second husband, the Honourable Francis Eveleigh de Moleyns. After Dorothy's death he continued the attempts to develop the estates as a commercial sporting venture.*
LEFT: *A 1950s advertisement for salmon fishing on the estates.*
OPPOSITE: *Weighing the catch outside the Balnagown Arms Hotel at Oykel Bridge in the late 1950s.*

1957 and was buried in the family vault in Kincardine churchyard, things were already slipping badly.

De Moleyns struggled on with further attempts to halt the losses. In 1958 a redevelopment plan for the estate's grouse moors was instituted and the moors at Benmore, Invercassley, Edderton and Scotsburn and Kincardine were taken in hand. But the losses continued to mount. The remaining rivers, shootings and the Bonar Fishing Station were sold at auction in 1961. The complex consortium of companies in the United States was dissolved in 1963 and the remaining lands and properties of Balnagown, now amounting to 60,000 acres (a tenth of their former extent) were vested in an Allied Bank of Ireland Trust.

In 1964 Francis de Moleyns died. The de Moleyns family continued for a time to live in part of the castle, while the rest stood empty and decaying. It was at this point that the Irish trust formed the Ross Estates Company to administer the estate and preserve the castle.

New Lairds: the Fayed Family

TOP: *Balnagown reborn. The castle was fully restored in the early 1990s. The different phases of construction over the centuries are clearly visible on the south front.*

ABOVE: *In the late 1960s the building was in a sorry state.*

OPPOSITE: *Mohamed Al Fayed with the Wallace Chair. The photograph shows the castle before the 1990s restoration, when the mock-masonry finish of the western parts was removed.*

IN 1972 BALNAGOWN CASTLE was sold to the Fayed family, who come originally from Alexandria in Egypt but have made their home in Britain. Mohamed Al Fayed, head of the family, had seen the castle by chance while driving past on a visit to the Dornoch Firth. He had been struck immediately by the romance of its antiquity. He discovered that it was for sale and bought it that same afternoon. Undaunted by the dilapidation of the building, he relished the challenge of restoring it. Soon after its acquisition, an extensive programme of renovation began and was completed in 1973.

Like their eighteenth-century Halkhead Ross predecessors, the present owners have been able to place Balnagown on a secure financial footing. In 1978 they acquired the remaining estates. Over the years other land has been added, and the total

acreage of the Balnagown Estates now stands at about twenty-three thousand acres, comprising four separate properties: Balnagown, Edderton and Ardgay are all in Easter Ross, while further north is the property around The Gorm and Duchally in Sutherland. Mohamed Al Fayed takes a considerable interest in the managing of the estates, which are all run along traditional lines with a mixture of farming and sporting use.

The landscapes are varied. Of the twenty-three thousand acres, about three thousand is given over to arable farming. This fertile farmland lies in Easter Ross, mostly on the property adjacent to Balnagown and Kildary, there is also useful farmland on the properties at Ardgay and Edderton near the Dornoch Firth to the north. More than a thousand acres of woodland is adjacent to Balnagown itself, continuing the tradition of forestation started by John Lockhart Ross in the

LEFT: *The unusual foot of the Principal Stairs with its wide, curving steps, exposed during restoration work.*
ABOVE LEFT: *A dormer gable of 1651 carved with the initials of the Twelfth Laird, David Ross, and his wife Mary Fraser. It is now concealed beneath a later roof. This photograph was taken during the recent restoration work.*
OPPOSITE: *The Red Stairs photographed during the 1990s restoration. The pendant vaulting of the first-floor landing is a good example of the castle's excellent Gothic Revival decoration.*

eighteenth century. There is some shooting on the estate at Balnagown and at Edderton a grouse moor is maintained, but the most significant sporting property lies further east: the deer forest on Benmore at The Gorm and Duchally in Strathcasseley extends over more than ten thousand acres.

At the castle itself an unexpected disaster struck in 1990. Damp had seeped through the external rendering, and the building was discovered to be badly affected by dry rot. An urgent rescue programme was implemented, and

over the following years the building underwent intensive restoration and reconstruction. Mohamed Al Fayed, who had already instituted historical restoration and conservation programmes at the Hôtel Ritz and at the former home of the Duke and Duchess of Windsor in Paris, as well as at Harrods in London, was well suited to the task. Few private individuals would have had the means or the courage to carry through the immense work necessary if the castle was to survive.

This second restoration programme brought

ABOVE: *Mohamed Al Fayed photographed in the Trophy Room. The Egyptian-born businessman, who has made his home in Britain, saved the castle from ruin after buying the property in 1972.*

LEFT: *The south front in 1992. Since this photograph was taken, the older parts of the castle have been harled in the course of the second restoration campaign.*

some unexpected advantages. In the course of the work structural deficiencies were discovered and put right. When a flimsy eighteenth-century partition wall by the main stairs was found to be acting as the only support for part of an upper storey, it was rebuilt and strengthened. The weak foundations of Gothic Revival east wing were also substantially reinforced.

Fortunately, there were still expert craftsmen available who were able to recreate the old workmanship in the interior. Looking today at the intricate plasterwork of the ceilings of the

Trophy Room and the Dining Room, it is hard to believe that these had to be virtually remade in the course of the restoration. The furniture, too, was repaired and refurbished.

At the end of this massive restoration work the castle stands more secure than it has done for many years. It is now a comfortable family home. The Fayed family is deeply committed to the historic heritage of their adopted country and proud of Balnagown's links with the Clan Ross. The mementoes of the old lairds, the Rosses and the Lockhart Rosses, are carefully preserved.

The Exterior

Balnagown Castle has grown in stages over the centuries, as can be seen from its irregular ground plan and the picturesque asymmetry of its exterior. Many people have had a hand in creating the building which we see today. Apart from John Adam in the eighteenth century, no professional architects are mentioned in the records. In the sixteenth and seventeenth centuries design and construction were often left to skilled craftsmen, but in the nineteenth century it was more unusual to dispense with an architect, as Lady Mary Ross did when she built the east wing.

The result is that Balnagown has preserved a quirky individuality far removed from the classicism of such nearby houses as New Tarbat House and Foulis Castle which were rebuilt in the eighteenth century. Balnagown's architecture and furnishings reflect the characters and personalities of many of its former lairds, as the styles of architecture of the various wings reflect the fashions of the day.

Approaching the castle from the west, along the drive that leads from the estate offices, through the steadings and past the castle's home farm (the Mains of Balnagown), the first view is of the oldest part of the building. The tall west wing is essentially the medieval tower-house probably built around 1490. From this angle the fortress-like character of the original castle is still evident. It was extended and raised in height around the turn of the seventeenth century, when John Nicolson is mentioned as master mason, and altered later in the century. The façade was given greater symmetry in the early nineteenth century when the turret at the north-west corner was added.

The walls are built of rubble stone covered with pink harling, the lime-wash roughcast characteristic of Scottish architecture. In the course of the recent restoration the rubble-stone walls have been covered again with, as it would have been originally. There is no limestone in the region, so the lime for the original harling would have been made by burning seashells over peat. Old photographs reveal that the exterior walls had undergone various treatments over the years: at different times parts had been rendered to simulate

RIGHT: *The bow in the centre of the south front was built in 1763. On the left is the gabled end of the old tower-house, while to the right the east wing built in the first half of the nineteenth century can be seen.*
LEFT: *Around the turn of the seventeenth century the original tower-house was reconstructed and extended to the north (on the left of the picture). The new extension included a turnpike staircase, now the oldest surviving in the castle.*

stonework, others had been stripped to the rubble stone beneath. The pinkish colour of the harling has given the building a cheerful air, emphasizing what the architectural historian John Gifford has called the 'endearingly lighthearted' character of Balnagown. Nevertheless the gun-loops in the lower parts of the walls, carefully uncovered and preserved in the restoration, are a reminder of its original defensive function.

The Gothic loggia in front of the ground floor here was one of the additions to the castle undertaken by Lady Mary Ross. It dates from 1818-21, when George Alexander, a builder-architect from Golspie in Sutherland, was engaged to remodel the west front. He also added the north-western turret, which was intended to balance its

seventeenth-century counterpart at the southern end and so make the west front more symmetrical.

The loggia incorporates two stone panels carved with the initials of Baron David Ross and his wife, Lady Anne Stewart. These date from their extensive alterations to the castle in the late seventeenth century. The panel in the centre with the Ross arms impaled with those of the Stewarts of Moray would almost certainly have graced the main entrance to the castle. Such an heraldic display was intended to proclaim immediately the ownership to all visitors. The carved panel above the archway at the northern end of this front includes the crests of the two families: the pelican of the Stewarts of Moray is in the top right-hand corner, while the crest of the Rosses, a hand grasping a laurel wreath, can be seen in the left-hand corner.

The recent removal of the southernmost bay of the nineteenth-century loggia, which was once linked to Lady Mary's now-vanished conservatory, has revealed the date 1600 incised on the corner stone. This part of the building must therefore belong to the alterations carried out for George Ross, the Ninth Laird, probably by the mason John Nicolson, around the beginning of the seventeenth century.

The driveway leads round to the south-facing entrance front where the

different stages of the growth of the castle can be clearly seen. To the left is the south side of the west wing. Evidence of its having been altered in the seventeenth century is the monogrammed stone dated 1672 with the intertwined initials of David Ross and Lady Anne set into the east-facing wall here.

In the centre of this front is projects a bow, part of John Lockhart Ross's addition to the castle, built in 1763, probably to designs by John Adam. Sir William Forbes described the result when he visited Balnagown in 1794: 'a large house, originally a Castle, with a Bow-window pieced to it . . .'

The battlemented parapet, the charming Gothic portico and the small conservatory on the right (which now serves as an entrance vestibule) were added by the Admiral's daughter-in-law, Lady Mary Ross, between 1832 and 1835, when this was made the main entrance to the castle. It is her coat of arms, the Ross arms impaled with the saltire cross of the Fitzgeralds, that is carved above the central archway. Portico and vestibule were built by James McBride, a carpenter and builder-architect from Elgin. The delicate ironwork tracery and curious battlemented caps to the columns (designed to hold the conical shrubs which complete the architectural effect) give the porch an appearance more oriental than Gothic. The effect is now

ABOVE LEFT: *The heraldic panel now in the centre of the nineteenth-century loggia on the west front contains the coats of arms of Ross and Stewart of Moray. In the seventeenth century it was usual for the arms of a castle's owners to be prominently displayed above the main entrance.*

ABOVE AND RIGHT: *The Gothic Revival entrance porch was added in the early 1830s. Above the entrance are the Ross arms impaled with the arms of the Fitzgeralds, Lady Mary Ross's family.*

enhanced by the two bronze beasts who flank the central doorway.

The larger conservatory which once adjoined the portico to the left can be seen in old photographs. It had fallen into disrepair and had to be demolished in 1972.

Like the west range, the eighteenth-century bow-fronted extension is built of rubble stone which has been harled during the restoration of 1992-95. The harling complements the warm reddish masonry of the Gothic Revival east wing built by Lady Mary between 1837 and 1841. The masons named in the building accounts for this part were James Rhind and Alexander Ross, the carpenter James McBride. Flanking the south front of this Gothic wing are two round towers with conical caps matching the turrets and bartizans on the west wing. Large pointed windows on the first and second floors, filled with cusped tracery of five and three lights respectively, give the exterior a somewhat ecclesiastical character – as Catherine Sinclair commented when she saw it newly built (see page 74).

The east and north fronts present more rugged appearance than the cheerful south front. Here the ground falls steeply away to the river below and the building rises above the tree-covered slope with a fortress-like air. The plain round tower at the north-east corner was built to take advantage of the fine views, as well as to add a vertical accent to the picturesque composition. The oldest parts of the north front date from the seventeenth century, but it was altered in the first half of the nineteenth century, and now presents has a confusing mixture of masonry of different periods. The initials 'SCR' (for Sir Charles Ross, the 'Jackdaw' laird) are carved on the first-floor oriel window added in the 1840s.

RIGHT: *An aerial photograph of the castle taken in the 1960s shows clearly the stages of the building's development from old tower-house (left), through the additions of the seventeenth and eighteenth centuries (centre) to the nineteenth-century Gothic east wing (right).*

The Interior

The interiors of Balnagown reflect many periods in the castle's history, though it is the nineteenth century that has left the greatest mark on the building. The medieval laird's hall with the vaulted chambers below are still recognizable, and there is a pleasant, airy eighteenth-century drawing room, as well as much fine Gothic Revival decoration.

The small **Entrance Hall** is tucked in between the curve of the bow front and the west side of the east wing. Its large windows and glazed ceiling reveal its original function: it is described as the 'small conservatory' in the building accounts.

This leads into a long room, now called the **Boot Room**. Its most unusual feature is hidden beneath the floor boards. A panel in front of the fireplace can be raised to reveal a sunken iron bath installed in the early nineteenth century by Lady Mary. In the short passageway leading from the boot room to the kitchen, two photographs of Tanganyika taken in the 1920s are a reminder of the big game safaris of the last Sir Charles Ross.

The Kitchen, on the ground floor of the east wing, has been thoroughly modernized in the recent restoration. The most striking original feature here is the oval window with heavy, cusped Gothic tracery.

At the foot of the Red Stairs, the secondary staircase built as part of the 1837-41 wing, a bronze plaque commemorates the use of the castle as a hospital during the First World War. Beyond the stairs, the staff sitting room occupies the north-eastern end of the castle, with the base of the round tower forming a circular room at one corner. The corridor leading westwards past offices and larders belongs to the late seventeenth-century extension of the castle. This section of the building was much altered by Lady Mary and her son in the first half of the nineteenth century. The cruciform windows, a playful version of medieval arrow-slits, are typical of the Romantic early Gothic Revival and reflect Lady Mary's taste for the castellated style.

RIGHT: *The Entrance Hall was built in the 1830s as the small conservatory attached to the south front.*

The late-sixteenth-century turnpike staircase in the north-west corner is probably part of the extension of the original castle built by George Ross. Traces of another turnpike staircase, with the spiral running the other way, have been discovered nearby. This would have been the original entrance staircase on the east side of the fifteenth-century tower-house.

The ground floor of the oldest part of the castle has the low, barrel-vaulted rooms usually found in medieval tower-houses. Since the entrance to the castle was on the first floor, these would have been inaccessible from the outside. They were built to be proof against attack and fire, and could also be used for storage or as dungeons. The thickness of the masonry and the arrow-slit in the wall here indicate that this was an external wall. During the restoration a defect in the eighteenth-century construction became apparent: the wall on the north side of the stairs, was too weak for its load-bearing function and had to be strengthened.

The **Main Hall**, the ground floor of Admiral John Lockhart Ross's extension. Today it is the main entrance to the castle. The room is still low, but its proportions are more generous than those of the medieval rooms, and it has large windows looking south.

It is not entirely clear how the rooms in the mid- eighteenth-century extension were originally used. John Gifford in his description of the castle in *The Buildings of Scotland* suggests that the Main Hall was formerly a dining room, with a drawing room on the floor above. A ground-floor dining room would have been convenient for access to the kitchens located on the north side of the castle. It has also been suggested that the present Drawing Room on the first floor was originally a dining room, and the present Master Bedroom was once a drawing room. Perhaps the two arrangements were both used at different times. In any case, this compact, vertical arrangement of rooms resembles that of a town house rather than of a country residence.

The Main Hall today contains a number of interesting pieces. On one wall hangs a large, eye-catching canvas by Edwin Long (1829-1891), an artist whose characteristic mix of religion and eroticism enjoyed immense popularity in his day. This work entitled *A Question of Propriety*, a version of a picture which Long displayed at the Royal Academy in 1875, now in the National Gallery of Victoria, Australia, shows a dancing girl performing before a bishop.

The elaborate walnut chimneypiece, its frieze carved with cavorting putti and festoons and supported by atlantides, is said to have been a gift from General John Kilpatrick, an officer in the Dutch service, when his daughter was betrothed to a Ross. Set into the wall above the mantelshelf are two seventeenth-century stone panels

OPPOSITE: *Dominating the Hall is Edwin Long's 'A Question of Propriety' painted in 1875.*

BELOW: *During the First World War Balnagown was used the British Red Cross as a military hospital. The commemorative brass plaque is now mounted on the wall of the Red Stairs.*

ABOVE: *The Main Hall today. When it was first built in the 1760s this was probably the dining room. It was not until the 1830s that this became the main entrance to the castle.*

LEFT: *The Hall in 1958, showing the portraits that hung there.*

OPPOSITE: *Above the handsome nineteenth-century walnut chimneypiece in the hall, a gift of John Kilpatrick, a general in the Dutch service, are two seventeenth-century panels carved in relief with biblical scenes.*

carved in bas relief with biblical scenes. The lower panel shows Jacob with Rachel at the well; the upper panel perhaps a scene from the story of Joseph. They were probably acquired in the nineteenth century.

The most important object in the room is the famous **Wallace Chair**, placed now beneath a fanciful nineteenth-century portrait of Sir William Wallace. Proclaimed Guardian of Scotland, he rallied the defeated Scots against the English occupiers at the end of the thirteenth century and met his death on an English gibbet. The chair is constructed of pine and has a deerskin cover. It is undoubtedly medieval, and may well have a connection with Wallace, since Lady Baillie-Ross, the wife of Admiral Sir John Lockhart Ross, was a lineal descendant of Wallace. Until the eighteenth century the chair stood in the Tower of Lamington in Lanarkshire, the ancestral home of Wallace's wife. In the nineteenth century the Lamington estates devolved on the elder daughter of General Sir Charles Ross, the Admiral's son, and the representation of Wallace passed to her son. The Chair, however, remained at Balnagown. It was taken by Sir Charles Ross to America for safety during the Second World War, and was later offered as a gift to Queen Elizabeth II. Her Majesty felt, however, that it was best retained in its present setting.

A notable feature of the **Principal Staircase** is the bottom pair of curved steps, which are unusually broad. The ceiling above the staircase has fine eighteenth-century plasterwork.

A glass case at the foot of the stairs contains stuffed golden eagles, the largest birds of prey in Scotland. These may have been birds which once lived in the large cage which stands in the grounds west of the castle.

On the first-floor landing, a door cut

ABOVE: *Lieutenant General John Kilpatrick (or Kirkpatrick), the donor of the Main Hall's chimneypiece, was governor of 'sHertogenbosch in the Netherlands. His portrait, by Adriaen Hanneman, formerly at Balnagown, is now in the Scottish National Gallery in Edinburgh.*

OPPOSITE: *The entrance to the Trophy Room through the massive walls of the old tower-house.*

through the four-foot thick wall (once the outer wall of the tower-house) leads to the **Trophy Room**. The room takes its present name from the many hunting trophies which line the walls: stags' heads from Scottish deer forests, and other more exotic beasts, including a lion, from the last Sir Charles Ross's hunting exploits further afield, in Africa, India and Russia.

Originally this was the laird's hall, the reception room of the medieval castle where the Chief of the Clan Ross would entertain and conduct clan business. It was much altered in the seventeenth and nineteenth centuries.

The room is dominated by the great seventeenth-century chimneypiece installed by Baron David Ross, the Thirteenth Laird, and his wife Lady Anne Stewart. This massive fireplace is the grandest display in the castle of the family pride of the Rosses. Like the heraldic carvings on the exterior of the castle, it is a declaration of ownership and a celebration the union of two powerful families. At the centre of the frieze above the mantelshelf are the coats of arms of the Chief and his wife, flanked by four heavy strapwork cartouches containing the initials of the couple both intertwined and separate.

A splendid addition to this heraldic display was made in the nineteenth century when a grate, fender and fire irons incorporating the Ross arms were installed. The two large brass figures of wild men, the Ross heraldic supporters, are particularly impressive.

In the recess in the wall to the left of the fireplace is an attractive nineteenth-century Scottish longcase clock with a face painted with costumed figures representing the seasons. The window in this embrasure was blocked when John Lockhart Ross built his extension in 1763. Around the blocked window are some very unusual wall paintings which apparently date from the late seventeenth century. The inscription on the curved soffit of the embrasure is from Psalm 74: OVR HELP IS IN [T]hE NAME OF ThE LORD / WhO MADE HEAVEN AND EARTh PS CXXIIII with the initials of Baron David Ross and Lady Anne Stewart. The dragon, wild beasts and a wild man with his club (a Ross heraldic supporter, or perhaps a local Highlander) may have been painted at the same time, though stylistically they are difficult to date. The use of religious inscriptions in domestic architecture was popular in

seventeenth-century Scotland. Fragments of painting can be seen in the window recess on the south wall, and remains of other inscriptions, which had been painted over, were found during restoration work above the northernmost window of the east wall, which was the original entrance door. These would have been part of a larger decorative programme for the whole room, which would probably have included one of the elaborately painted ceilings typical of Scottish palaces and castles in this period.

The present magnificent plaster ceiling, painted to resemble wood, with its splendid circular roses, was installed in the nineteenth century. Like other ceilings in the castle, it had to be completely removed and remade in the 1990s restoration. Two skilled craftsmen were brought out of retirement to supervise the casting of the intricate designs. Carved wooden pelmets above the windows incorporating the Ross crest and motto (SPEM SUCCESSUS ALIT: 'Success Nourishes Hope'), now draped with Ross tartan, were also made for the room in the nineteenth century.

Framed on the wall next to the recess with the inscription are some of the most interesting documents from the Balnagown archives. As well as a photographic reproduction of the charter from King Robert II in 1375 confirming his nephew William Ross, the second laird, in his ownership of Balnagown (the original is on loan to the Scottish Record Office in Edinburgh), several of the items recall events from the turbulent years of

RIGHT: *The nineteenth-century plaster ceiling of the Trophy Room, with its painted wood-graining, has been meticulously restored.*

ABOVE: *The great heraldic chimneypiece at the south end of the Trophy Room was installed by the Thirteenth Laird, Baron David Ross, and his wife Lady Anne Stewart. Their arms appear side by side between their intertwined initials. In spite of financial difficulties the couple continued to build in a 'large and nobel manner'.*

LEFT: *Signatures from Balnagown documents. In the centre is Lady Anne Stewart's careful script, with the flowing signature of her husband, David Ross, and that of Lord Ross (here spelt 'Rosse') of Halkhead.*

OPPOSITE, CENTRE AND ABOVE: *The mysterious paintings in the window recess show a dragon, a wild cat and a Highlander beneath a biblical inscription. The remains of painted decoration can also be found in the recess left of the fireplace.*

the sixteenth and seventeenth centuries:

An instrument of revocation (in Latin) in 1562 from three canons of Fearn Abbey claiming that they had ceded land to Alexander Ross under duress.

A Decree in Council of 1586 confirming that Alexander Ross had been deprived of Balnagown Castle and its lands because of his lawlessness and that they had been given to his son George.

A letter of 1598 from King James VI to George Ross thanking him for quartering some soldiers at the castle.

A letter of March 1639 from the Earl of Sutherland urging David Ross, the Twelfth Laird, to have his people in readiness to support the Covenanters' cause.

A letter of June 1639 from Earl Marischal and the Earl of Montrose, asking David Ross for forces to be ready to fight against the Gordons. Montrose was commanding forces of the Covenanters.

A letter of 1651 from King Charles II to David Ross, calling on him to muster his clansmen and meet at Aberdeen to march south and restore the king to his English throne.

An inventory of furniture at Balnagown made in 1719 after the death of Lady Anne Stewart, widow of David Ross, the Thirteenth Laird.

In a frame on the opposite wall, near the passage to the Gun Room, is the voluminous marriage contract drawn up between General Sir Charles Ross and his second wife Lady Mary Fitzgerald in 1799.

The Trophy Room also contains mementoes of the General's illustrious father, Admiral Sir John Lockhart Ross: an engraving of the portrait painted by Sir Joshua Reynolds in 1762, and, in the window embrasure to the left of the fireplace, a rather inaccurate model of the French ship the *Mélampe*, the vessel of thirty-six guns which he captured in 1757, one of the many

prizes which brought him fame and a considerable fortune.

Opposite the fireplace a large Art Nouveau stained glass panel from the turn of the present century depicts a maiden carrying fruit. To the left of this a passageway cutting through the four-foot-thick wall leads to the **Gun Room**. The thickness of this wall is a clue to the history of the building here: the Gun Room is part of the late sixteenth century addition to the castle built by George Ross. Painted on the ceiling of the gun room the Ross coat of arms appears once again. The weapons displayed here are more antiquated than the Ross Rifle which made Sir Charles's name at the turn of the century, but the room is a reminder of the important part that hunting played in the lives of the last two lairds. On the walls here hang two colourful portraits, one is of Dorothy, Lady Ross, the last Sir Charles's widow, and the other of her second husband Francis de Moleyns. The portrait of Lady Ross shows the castle in the background. The paintings are of interest as early works by Tom Keating, the maverick painter who was later to gain notoriety for fooling the art world with his pastiches of Samuel Palmer. A rowing oar from the Cambridge Eight in which the last Sir Charles Ross rowed in the 1894 University Boat Race, is also displayed here.

The main doorway on the first-floor landing of the Principal Staircase has an archway carved in grey stone with intricate foliage patterns. The workmanship is not local: the style of carving is unlike any Scottish work. The archway was probably made in Germany in the seventeenth century, and was brought to Balnagown in the nineteenth century, when it was incorporated into the alterations to the castle. The wooden panels of the door were created then to match the stone

ABOVE: *The Mélampe, a French frigate sent in 1757 to pursue Captain Lockhart's cruiser the Tartar, became his most celebrated prize. This somewhat inaccurate model of the ship (in fact, she carried thirty-six guns) is displayed in the Trophy Room.*

OPPOSITE: *What is now the Gun Room was originally built in the sixteenth century as a smaller private room leading off the laird's hall.*

carving. On the wall above the archway the Ross arms appear once again.

The archway leads to the **Music Room**. This was part of the seventeenth-century castle, but was later given the white and gold Gothic interior decoration favoured by Lady Mary Ross in her alterations. The room accommodates the adjoining spiral staircase, which gives it a curious piano-like shape. This is perhaps an indication that Lady Mary did not use a professional architect for her alterations to the castle; an architect of the stature of James Gillespie Graham would certainly have attempted to introduce more regularity into the plan.

However, the decorative detailing here and elsewhere in the Gothic Revival interiors shows that craftsmen of the highest calibre were employed.

The adjoining **Library** was

ABOVE: *The wall of the Music Room curves round the turnpike staircase next door.*
OPPOSITE: *The arched doorway to the Music Room is probably seventeenth-century German work.*

redecorated by Lady Mary in the same delicate neo-Gothic style, with a flat ceiling criss-crossed by plaster vaulting ribs. Like the Music Room, this was part of the castle built in the seventeenth century by David Ross and Lady Anne Stewart. Hanging above the nineteeth century Gothic fireplace, is a state portrait of Charles II, after Sir Peter Lely, a reminder of the loyalty which the Twelfth and Thirteenth Lairds showed their sovereign in the difficult years of the Commonwealth. On the opposite wall another Lely portrait shows King Charles's sister-in-law, Mary of Modena, the consort of James VII (and II). It is surprising to find this portrait of the mother of the Old Pretender at Balnagown, since the Rosses were anti-Jacobite.

The oriel window looks out on to one of the finest inland views in this part of Scotland, along the Balnagown River to the wooded hills beyond. It, too, was added in the mid-nineteenth century. The window bay has fine rib vaulting in plaster. The most striking piece of

LEFT: *A state portrait of Mary of Modena, the consort of King James VII (James II of England), by the studio of Sir Peter Lely, hangs in the Library.* ABOVE: *A detail of the portrait, showing the inscription.*

furniture in the room is a Victorian giltwood screen with five glazed panels each enclosing Dresden porcelain plates.

A wide opening through the thickness of the seventeenth-century walls leads to the **Drawing Room**, part of John Lockhart Ross's addition to the castle, perhaps built by John Adam. As we have seen, the room may have undergone a change in function since it was built. It is possible that in the early nineteenth century it was used as a dining room, with a buffet recess where the entrance through to the Library now is, and that at that time the drawing room was the room directly above (now the Master Bedroom).

The room was altered in the early nineteenth century, but it was not gothicized and still reflects in its plain classical form something of the enlightened, matter-of-fact character of the Admiral. Its large windows in the

ABOVE: *The bay-window in the Library was inserted to take advantage of the spectacular views along the river. The nineteenth-century giltwood screen incorporates Dresden porcelain plates.*

OPPOSITE: *The Library, like the Music Room, was given its Gothic Revival decoration in the second quarter of the nineteenth century. Over the fireplace hangs a state portrait, after Sir Peter Lely, of King Charles II, who granted the Thirteenth Laird an annual pension of £200 in gratitude for services rendered by his father in 1651.*

south-facing bow look out over the park.

According to the Victorian architectural writer Robert Kerr, dining rooms should have 'masculine importance', drawing rooms 'feminine delicacy'. Something of this division of domains within the house can be felt at Balnagown. The exquisite inlaid Carrara marble chimneypiece, with a festooned classical medallion in the middle, is a fine example of the delicate neo-classical style promoted by the Adam brothers.

On the wall opposite the fireplace is a large group portrait of Sir William Gordon, the founder of the port of Invergordon, and his family, painted by Richard Waitt, who was active in the first quarter of the eighteenth century. Waitt specialized in still-life and in characterful portraits of Highland

ABOVE: *This family portrait of Sir William and Lady Gordon of Invergordon with their children is one of the most charming in the Balnagown collection. The artist, Richard Waitt, painted many portraits of Highland lairds in the early eighteenth century. Sir William founded Invergordon, a few miles from Balnagown, as a fishing village in the mid-eighteenth century.*

LEFT: *The portrait above the fireplace in the Drawing Room is attributed to William Aikman and probably shows Sir William's eldest son, John, later to become Secretary of State for Scotland.*

OPPOSITE: *The pair of nineteenth-century gilt bronze statuettes in the Drawing Room represent characters from Sir Walter Scott's novels. Scott's friend and amanuensis, William Laidlaw, was the factor at Balnagown in the 1830s.*

lairds. It is hard to believe that this can be the family portrait which struck Catherine Sinclair on her visit to the castle in 1840, although the sitters were the same:

> One [painting] which attracted much of our attention, represented Sir William Gordon taking leave of his wife and seven children, previous to going abroad, the whole party being in tears! An odd moment to choose for sitting, and certainly not a happy one! Matthews used to exhibit seven different ways of laughing, and here may be seen as many styles of weeping! One of the young ladies, who was evidently handsome, afterwards became Countess of Cromarty.

It was the eldest of the daughters, Isabella, celebrated as 'Bonny Bell Gordon', who married the 3rd Earl of Cromartie. Her petitions saved her husband's life after he was sentenced to death for his part in the Jacobite rising.

The portrait of the boy above the fireplace is attributed to William Aikman. The identity of the boy, who holds a rod in his right hand, while rejecting the toys of childhood with his left, is uncertain, but comparison with the Gordon family portrait suggests he is probably the eldest son, John Gordon.

These portraits may possibly have come to the castle in the eighteenth century through Admiral Sir John Lockhart Ross's wife, whose stepmother was one of the Gordon daughters in the painting. The naval portrait by the door shows John Lockhart Ross himself. Although the facial features in this portrait seem to differ slightly from other known pictures of the Admiral, the pose is very similar to the portraits of him by Reynolds and Zoffany.

The large blue and gold Chinese Peking carpet, decorated with prunus,

peonies and bats, belongs to the late nineteenth-century furnishing of the room, and is one of a number of oriental items acquired at that time. The fine crystal chandeliers in the Drawing Room and Music Room also date from the nineteenth century.

Beyond the Drawing Room is the **Gallery**, one of the most enchanting interiors in the castle. This passageway with plaster Gothic rib-vaulting in white and gold runs from the front to the back of the castle. The most

LEFT: *The Gallery, with its plaster rib-vaulting, runs from north to south between the older part of the castle and the nineteenth-century east wing.*

ABOVE: *Among the marble sculpture that lines the Gallery is this striking bust, carved in 1930 by the American sculptor Moses Dykaar, of the last Sir Charles Ross dressed for safari.*

arresting of the marble busts and portraits which line its walls is without doubt the head-and-shoulders bust of the last Sir Charles Ross, carved by the American sculptor Moses Dykaar in 1930 (the year of Ross's notorious divorce from his second wife). Showing the baronet dressed as a hunter, with a bush shirt and ten rifle rounds on his chest, the bust captures something of his malignant genius. Above it hangs a portrait of his grandfather General Sir Charles Ross, by Sir James Watson Gordon, and nearby is a painting of his third wife, Dorothy. In front of the window at one end stands one of the finest of the many nineteenth-century Italian Carrara marble sculptures which adorn the castle, *Venus at her Bath*, by A. Piazza.

The **Dining Room**, the most magnificent of the castle's Gothic Revival interiors, is reached through a doorway on the left at the southern end of the Gallery. One slightly discordant note in the otherwise Gothic decoration is the white marble chimneypiece. Its bulging volutes and floral carving belong to the world of the Baroque. The vaulted bay window embrasure is surmounted by an ogee-arched panel enclosing the Ross arms, and the detailing within the corner turrets is also of exceptional quality) But the most impressive feature of the room is the superb fan-vaulted ceiling with its pendant boss. The whole ceiling had to be taken down and remade during the latest restoration.

The wallpaper, which forms an integral part of the decoration, had also badly deteriorated. The accounts reveal that in 1840 it was hung for £25, the cost of materials being £4 4s 5d. However, the expense of replacing it in the 1990s with a specially made replica was of course considerably greater. The red, gold and cream pattern was accurately reproduced, though without the flock finish of the original.

The oak furniture was made for the room around 1860 in a

ABOVE: *Charles Goldsborough Anderson's striking portrait of Rebecca, Lady Ross, the mother of the last baronet, hangs above the Dining Room fireplace. It was painted in 1900.*

RIGHT: *The Gothic Revival Dining Room, with its rib-vaulting and unusual window tracery, is one of the castle's most impressive interiors. The quality of the decoration is excellent, but certain features – the non-alignment of the ridge-rib and the pointed window, for example – suggest that a professional architect was not employed.*

heavy, High Victorian classical style. The oak table and sideboards, one of them prominently decorated with the Ross arms, are good examples of the period. The ensemble may have been commissioned by the penultimate Sir Charles or his second wife, Rebecca, whom he married in 1865.

The portraits in this room are of exceptional interest. They show the leading characters in the history of the castle in the nineteenth and early twentieth centuries. Flanking the window bay are a pair of three-quarter-length portraits by the precocious Scottish painter, Andrew Somerville (1808-1834), best known for his paintings of Border ballads and rural life, who died at the age of twenty-six before he could fulfil his early promise. On the left is Lady Mary Ross, who looks an amiable woman. She is depicted with her horse, which turns its head appealingly to the spectator. The matching portrait on the right is of her unfortunate son, Sir Charles, the eccentric Eighth Baronet. He is shown here as a young man out with his lurcher, an indication of his lifelong love of the outdoors and hunting.

Above the mantelshelf is a full-length portrait of his widow, Rebecca. It was painted in 1900 by Charles Goldsborough Anderson, a few years after she was driven from the house by her son, the last Sir Charles Ross of Balnagown. He himself appears on the adjoining wall in a swaggering full-length portrait by Charles Hardie painted in 1894 to celebrate the attainment of his majority. The arrogant young laird is shown in a very different style to his his more retiring father standing on a hillside in full Highland costume, and wearing in his hat the three eagle feathers traditionally reserved for the Clan Chief, with a deerhound at his feet.

The first-floor landing of the Red Staircase has another fine Gothic Revival plaster ceiling. A few steps up on the left is a room now used as the **Study**, formerly the Billiard Room. The late-nineteenth-century oak chimneypiece is decorated with delightful medieval-style tiles depicting the seasons. A doorway in the corner of the room leads to the round tower at the north-east corner of the castle.

On the second floor the **Master Bedroom** contains one of the most remarkable pieces in the castle. This is a mid-sixteenth-century sandstone chimneypiece brought here in the last century from Meikle Daan, a fortified house, once a Ross residence but now ruined, which stands a few miles to the north overlooking the Dornoch Firth. The frieze below the mantel-shelf records the marriage of Hector Munro, the minister of Edderton, and Euphemia Ross, daughter of William Ross of Invercharron. Between two semicircles containing profile faces, perhaps representing the sun and moon, are three roundels. In the middle roundel is the figure of the minister in his Geneva hat and cloak. He holds an open book with the text

ABOVE: The magnificent Gothic oak bed, carved with the Ross arms, was commissioned for the new east wing in the mid-nineteenth century. LEFT: The chimneypiece in the Study has a surround made up of late nineteenth-century tiles illustrating the seasons of the year based on images from medieval manuscript illumination.

ABOVE: *The mid-sixteenth-century carved sandstone chimneypiece brought to Balnagown in the nineteenth century from nearby Meikle Daan.*
RIGHT: *A nineteenth-century Chinese silk hanging, decorated with delicate embroidery, adorns a wall on the Principal Stairs.*

FEAR GOD IN HEART AS YE MAY BE B[les]S[e]D. Around him are the initials MHM (Magister Hector Munro) and ER (Euphemia Ross) and the motto SERVIRE DEO EST REGNARE ('To serve God is to rule'). The roundel on the left contains the arms of the Munros, an eagle's head, with their motto AQUILA NON CÀPTAT MUSCAS ('An eagle does not catch flies'), and that on the right the Ross arms with the familiar three lions but an unfamiliar motto: NOB[i]LIS EST IRA LEONIS ('Noble is the anger of the lion'). When Alexander Munro, Hector's descendant, married

Margaret Forester in 1680, their initials (AMMF) were added to the lintel stone, with the date and the motto SOLI DEO GLORIA ('To God alone be glory'). This unique carving has undergone meticulous cleaning and conservation in the recent restoration programme.

The delightful Gothic Revival furniture commissioned in the mid-nineteenth century for the new interiors includes a spectacular four-poster bed with crenellated tester and a headboard carved with the Ross arms.

The Garden and Grounds

The castle policies (grounds) have undergone many changes in the last five centuries. In the early days, when defence was the priority and the surrounding landscape was wilder than it is today, the castle's inhabitants had no need of pleasure gardens. It was not until the seventeenth century, in more peaceful times, that gardens were created for recreation. At some time before the mid-eighteenth century a bowling green was laid out on the flat land to the south of the castle.

John Lockhart Ross transformed the grounds around the castle when he made Balnagown his residence in the 1760s. He landscaped the grounds, creating a pleasant park and a large walled garden between the the domestic offices and the castle, as well as repairing the river bank and introducing new drainage.

The next major contribution came from Lady Mary Ross in the early part of the nineteenth century, reflecting the fashionable sensibility for the Picturesque landscape. Traces of her garden layout can still be seen. Winding walks were provided for visitors along paths laid out along the banks and under the woods by the river. In 1822 seven small bridges were built, at a cost of six shillings each, to take the paths over damp hollows.

A marble plaque on the slope overlooking the river below the castle to the east records the creation by Lady Mary's daughter-in-law, Elizabeth, of the Italian Gardens by the river. They were completed at Christmas 1847, a few months before her premature death. The steep slopes down to the river from the castle were terraced. Flights of stone steps with ornamental plinths led down to the lawns below, where parterres were laid out, decorated with rustic arches

LEFT: *The Steadings to the west of the castle built in the late eighteenth century.*

OVER: *A picture postcard of around 1910 shows the Italian Gardens with their fountain and pergolas.*

An Autumn View of a corner of Italian Garden

ns, Balnagown, from the North

covered with climbing roses. A fountain stood at the centre. The river banks were edged with dark Italian firs, marble statues were dispersed over the lawns and seats placed for visitors to admire the views.

A path ran from the entrance gate by the river to a pool hewn out of the rocky cliff face. This was fed by an inlet from the river and bridged to a small island in the centre, which was shaded by enormous leafy trees. Carved on the cliff here the initials 'SCR' (for Sir Charles Ross) can still be seen. A well was bored to provide fresh water for the castle.

For centuries the river was used not only for recreation but also as a source of power. Beyond the King's Bridge a mill-race had long existed, providing energy for a sawmill and laundry. In 1888 a turbine was installed here to generate electricity.

The small one-storey building above the terraces of the Italian Gardens belongs to an ice-house dating from the early nineteenth century, with underground chambers for storing ice. Before the days of refrigeration, this was essential in the summer months, especially for storing fish from rivers on the estate.

The Eagles' Cage in the field next to the castle was erected in the nineteenth century, when a golden eagle was kept here. Its keeper had to provide 'three pairs of rabbits each week to be fed to the eagle, else it had to be fed mutton.' Golden eagle feathers are the traditional emblems of clan chiefdom: the last of the Lockhart Rosses regarded himself as a Chief, wearing three feathers in his bonnet.

The estate records show that in 1861 a staff of twenty-four was employed to care for the policies, the gardens and the laundry. At that time the daily pay was 6 pence for women

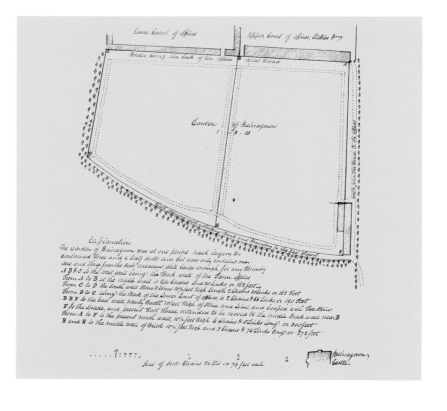

and one shilling for men – at the end of the year they received a bonus of an extra shilling and a nip of whisky.

During the later nineteenth century, when, Rebecca Ross was running the estate, the gardens were kept in good repair and further

ABOVE: *Walks along the picturesque banks of the Balnagown River were first created by Lady Mary Ross in the early nineteenth century.*

LEFT: *This plan of the large walled garden to the west of the castle was drawn in 1810, when alterations were made.*

RIGHT: *A view down to the site of the Italian Gardens.*

LEFT: *The natural beauty of the Balnagown River is enhanced by the landscaped gardens.*

ABOVE: *A view up from the riverside lawns to the terraces below the castle.*

enriched. The river banks were planted with rhododendrons and other flowering shrubs. A lean-to greenhouse was built in the walled gardens to grow peaches and grapes.

Evidence of the ingenious and innovative mind of Rebecca's son, the last Sir Charles, can also be seen in the garden: the stone foundations of his workshops built by the river for the heavy machinery used in his projects and the manufacture of agricultural implements. The stables were converted to garages, for Sir Charles owned one of the first Benz cars and later a Humber. He was active in the re-seeding and draining of unproductive ground. 'My castle green', he wrote, 'has become a correct and profitable lambing field, and is no longer a rabbit warren and a pheasant covert.' During his later years and after his death, however, the grounds were allowed to decline and the walled garden was neglected.

The attractive Steadings belong to the time of agricultural improvement around the end of the eighteenth century. They form three sides of a picturesque quadrangle, with the west range comprising a fine pedimented stable block. Today the Steadings have been converted to accommodation for staff and guests.

Family Trees

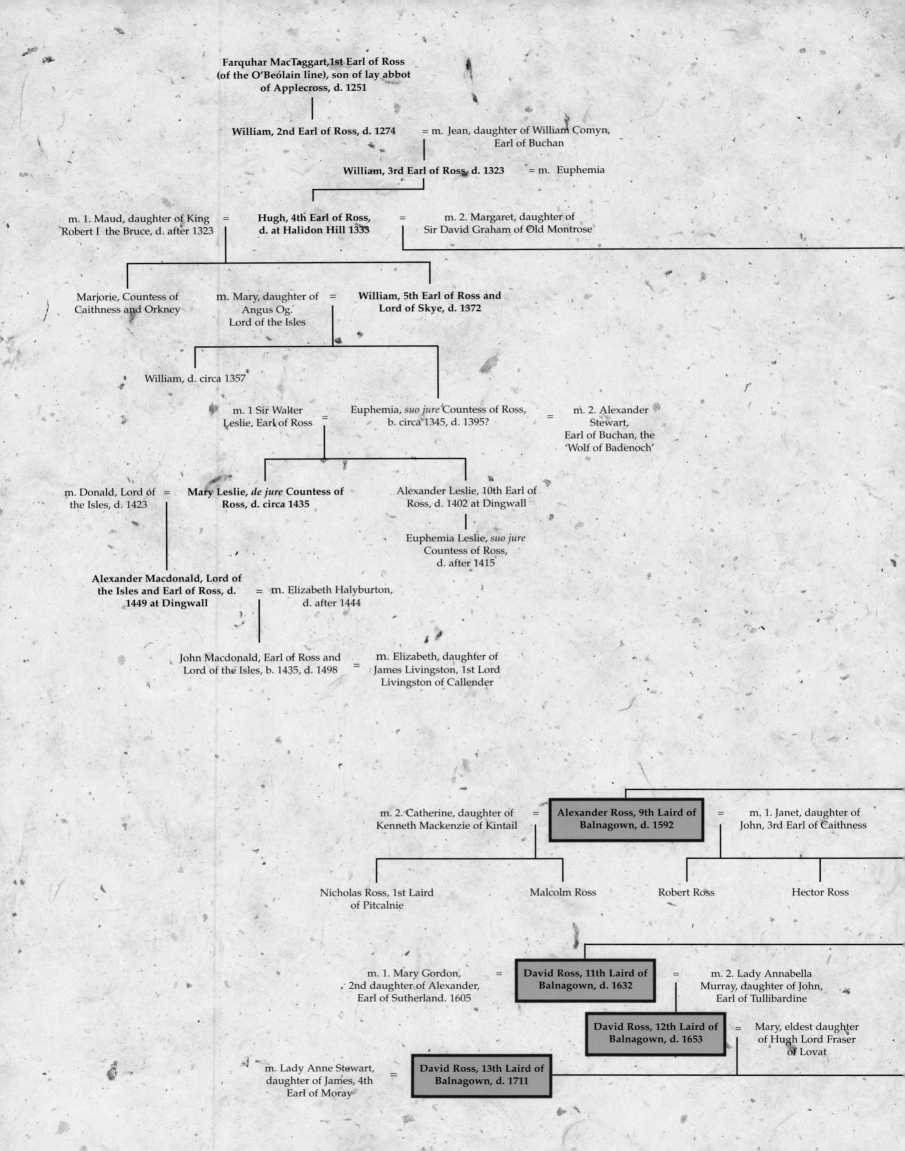

Farquhar MacTaggart, 1st Earl of Ross
(of the O'Beolain line), son of lay abbot
of Applecross, d. 1251

William, 2nd Earl of Ross, d. 1274 = m. Jean, daughter of William Comyn, Earl of Buchan

William, 3rd Earl of Ross, d. 1323 = m. Euphemia

m. 1. Maud, daughter of King = Hugh, 4th Earl of Ross, = m. 2. Margaret, daughter of
Robert I the Bruce, d. after 1323   d. at Halidon Hill 1333   Sir David Graham of Old Montrose

Marjorie, Countess of   m. Mary, daughter of = William, 5th Earl of Ross and
Caithness and Orkney   Angus Og.   Lord of Skye, d. 1372
                            Lord of the Isles

William, d. circa 1357

m. 1 Sir Walter = Euphemia, *suo jure* Countess of Ross, = m. 2. Alexander
Leslie, Earl of Ross   b. circa 1345, d. 1395?   Stewart,
                                                             Earl of Buchan, the
                                                             'Wolf of Badenoch'

m. Donald, Lord of = Mary Leslie, *de jure* Countess of   Alexander Leslie, 10th Earl of
the Isles, d. 1423   Ross, d. circa 1435   Ross, d. 1402 at Dingwall

                                                           Euphemia Leslie, *suo jure*
                                                           Countess of Ross,
                                                           d. after 1415

Alexander Macdonald, Lord of
the Isles and Earl of Ross, d. = m. Elizabeth Halyburton,
1449 at Dingwall   d. after 1444

John Macdonald, Earl of Ross and = m. Elizabeth, daughter of
Lord of the Isles, b. 1435, d. 1498   James Livingston, 1st Lord
                                      Livingston of Callender

m. 2. Catherine, daughter of = **Alexander Ross, 9th Laird of** = m. 1. Janet, daughter of
Kenneth Mackenzie of Kintail   **Balnagown, d. 1592**   John, 3rd Earl of Caithness

Nicholas Ross, 1st Laird   Malcolm Ross   Robert Ross   Hector Ross
of Pitcalnie

m. 1. Mary Gordon, = **David Ross, 11th Laird of** = m. 2. Lady Annabella
2nd daughter of Alexander, **Balnagown, d. 1632**   Murray, daughter of John,
Earl of Sutherland. 1605   Earl of Tullibardine

                            David Ross, 12th Laird of = Mary, eldest daughter
                            Balnagown, d. 1653   of Hugh Lord Fraser
                                                            of Lovat

m. Lady Anne Stewart, = **David Ross, 13th Laird of**
daughter of James, 4th   **Balnagown, d. 1711**
Earl of Moray

The Balnagown Ancestry and Inheritance
Earls of Ross and Rosses of Balnagown
(Lairds of Balnagown are highlighted in blue)

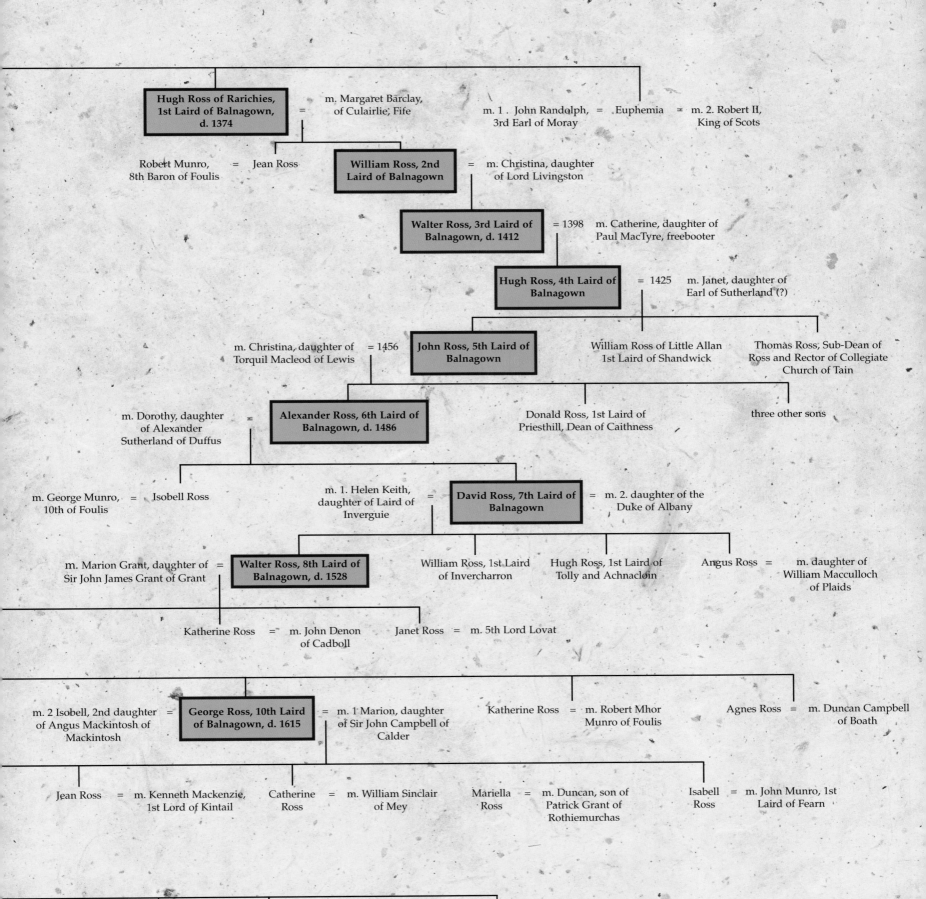

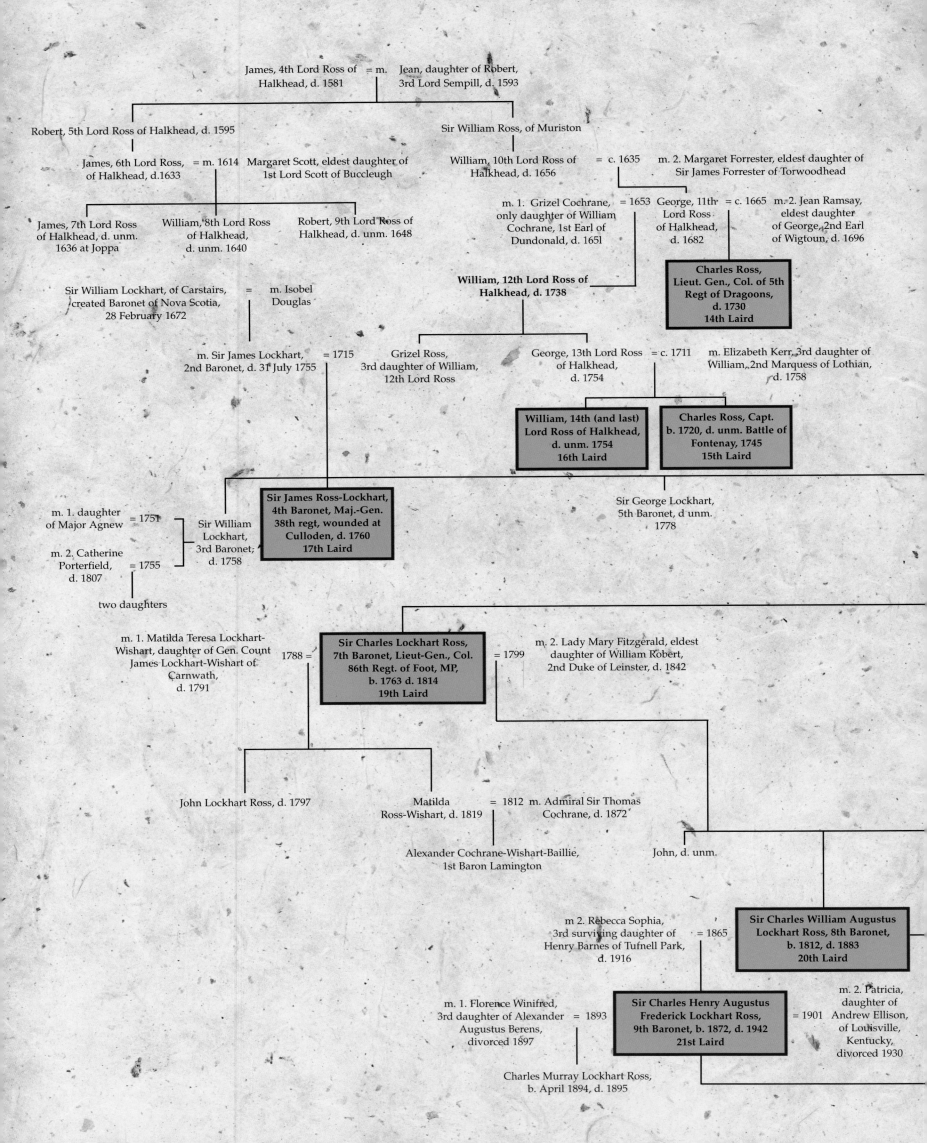

James, 4th Lord Ross of Halkhead, d. 1581 = m. Jean, daughter of Robert, 3rd Lord Sempill, d. 1593

Robert, 5th Lord Ross of Halkhead, d. 1595

Sir William Ross, of Muriston

James, 6th Lord Ross, of Halkhead, d.1633 = m. 1614 Margaret Scott, eldest daughter of 1st Lord Scott of Buccleugh

William, 10th Lord Ross of Halkhead, d. 1656 = c. 1635 m. 2. Margaret Forrester, eldest daughter of Sir James Forrester of Torwoodhead

James, 7th Lord Ross of Halkhead, d. unm. 1636 at Joppa

William, 8th Lord Ross of Halkhead, d. unm. 1640

Robert, 9th Lord Ross of Halkhead, d. unm. 1648

m. 1. Grizel Cochrane, only daughter of William Cochrane, 1st Earl of Dundonald, d. 1651 = 1653 George, 11th Lord Ross of Halkhead, d. 1682 = c. 1665 m. 2. Jean Ramsay, eldest daughter of George, 2nd Earl of Wigtoun, d. 1696

Charles Ross, Lieut. Gen., Col. of 5th Regt of Dragoons, d. 1730 14th Laird

Sir William Lockhart, of Carstairs, created Baronet of Nova Scotia, 28 February 1672 = m. Isobel Douglas

William, 12th Lord Ross of Halkhead, d. 1738

m. Sir James Lockhart, 2nd Baronet, d. 31 July 1755 = 1715 Grizel Ross, 3rd daughter of William, 12th Lord Ross

George, 13th Lord Ross of Halkhead, d. 1754 = c. 1711 m. Elizabeth Kerr, 3rd daughter of William, 2nd Marquess of Lothian, d. 1758

William, 14th (and last) Lord Ross of Halkhead, d. unm. 1754 16th Laird

Charles Ross, Capt. b. 1720, d. unm. Battle of Fontenay, 1745 15th Laird

m. 1. daughter of Major Agnew = 1751

Sir William Lockhart, 3rd Baronet; d. 1758

Sir James Ross-Lockhart, 4th Baronet, Maj.-Gen. 38th regt, wounded at Culloden, d. 1760 17th Laird

Sir George Lockhart, 5th Baronet, d unm. 1778

m. 2. Catherine Porterfield, d. 1807 = 1755

two daughters

m. 1. Matilda Teresa Lockhart-Wishart, daughter of Gen. Count James Lockhart-Wishart of Carnwath, d. 1791 1788 =

Sir Charles Lockhart Ross, 7th Baronet, Lieut-Gen., Col. 86th Regt. of Foot, MP, b. 1763 d. 1814 19th Laird

= 1799 m. 2. Lady Mary Fitzgerald, eldest daughter of William Robert, 2nd Duke of Leinster, d. 1842

John Lockhart Ross, d. 1797

Matilda Ross-Wishart, d. 1819 = 1812 m. Admiral Sir Thomas Cochrane, d. 1872

Alexander Cochrane-Wishart-Baillie, 1st Baron Lamington

John, d. unm.

m. 2. Rebecca Sophia, 3rd surviving daughter of Henry Barnes of Tufnell Park, d. 1916 = 1865

Sir Charles William Augustus Lockhart Ross, 8th Baronet, b. 1812, d. 1883 20th Laird

m. 1. Florence Winifred, 3rd daughter of Alexander Augustus Berens, divorced 1897 = 1893

Sir Charles Henry Augustus Frederick Lockhart Ross, 9th Baronet, b. 1872, d. 1942 21st Laird

m. 2. Patricia, daughter of Andrew Ellison, of Louisville, Kentucky, divorced 1930 = 1901

Charles Murray Lockhart Ross, b. April 1894, d. 1895

The Balnagown Inheritance
Rosses of Halkhead and Lockhart Rosses

(Lairds of Balnagown are highlighted in blue)

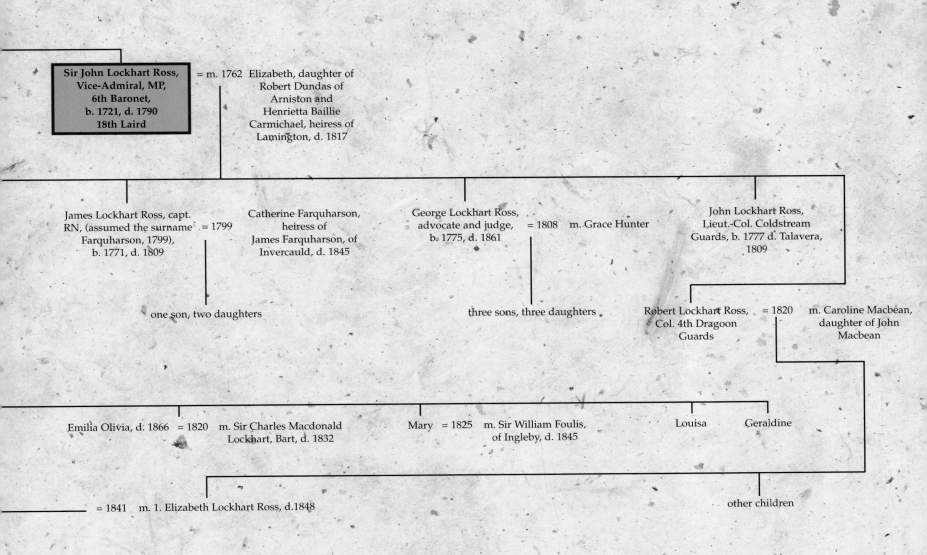

**Sir John Lockhart Ross,
Vice-Admiral, MP,
6th Baronet,
b. 1721, d. 1790
18th Laird** = m. 1762 Elizabeth, daughter of Robert Dundas of Arniston and Henrietta Baillie Carmichael, heiress of Lamington, d. 1817

James Lockhart Ross, capt. RN, (assumed the surname Farquharson, 1799), b. 1771, d. 1809 = 1799 Catherine Farquharson, heiress of James Farquharson, of Invercauld, d. 1845

George Lockhart Ross, advocate and judge, b. 1775, d. 1861 = 1808 m. Grace Hunter

John Lockhart Ross, Lieut.-Col. Coldstream Guards, b. 1777 d. Talavera, 1809

one son, two daughters

three sons, three daughters

Robert Lockhart Ross, Col. 4th Dragoon Guards = 1820 m. Caroline Macbean, daughter of John Macbean

Emilia Olivia, d. 1866 = 1820 m. Sir Charles Macdonald Lockhart, Bart, d. 1832

Mary = 1825 m. Sir William Foulis, of Ingleby, d. 1845

Louisa

Geraldine

= 1841 m. 1. Elizabeth Lockhart Ross, d.1848

other children

= 1939 m. 3. **Dorothy Mercado, Lady Ross, d. 1957** = 1953 m. 2. **The Hon. Francis Eveleigh de Moleyns, d. 1960**

Bibliography

Bain, Robert *History of the Ancient Province of Ross,* Dingwall 1899

Campbell, John *The Naval History of Great Britain*, vol. 6, London 1818,
        (pp. 350–369: 'Sir John Lockhart Ross, Bart, Vice-Admiral of the Blue')

Gifford, John *Highland and Islands* (The Buildings of Scotland), London 1992

Howard, Deborah *Scottish Architecture from the Reformation to the Restoration*, Edinburgh 1995

Macgill, W. *Old Ross-shire and Scotland as seen in the Tain and Balnagown Documents*, Inverness 1909,
        and 1911 (Supplementary Volume)

Macgill, W. 'The "Breve Cronicle of the Erllis of Ross"', *Transactions of the Glasgow Archaeological Society,*
        N.S., vol VII, part III (1924) pp. 313–329

Mackinnon, Donald *The Clan Ross*, Edinburgh 1957

Maclean, Fitzroy *Highlanders: A History of the Scottish Clans*, London 1995

Meldrum, Helen Myers *Kilmuir Easter: The History of a Highland Village,* Inverness 1935

Pridham, C.H.B. *Superiority of Fire,* London 1945

Ross, Alexander M. *History of the Clan Ross, with Genealogies of the Various Families,* Dingwall 1932

Ross, John Robert, et al. *The Great Clan Ross*, Orillia, Ontario, Canada 1993 (3rd edition)

Sinclair, Catherine *Scotland and the Scotch, or The Western Circuit,* Edinburgh 1840

Taylor, William *History of Tain*, Tain 1882

Tranter, Nigel *The Queen's Scotland: The North-East*, London 1974

Colvin, Howard *A Biographical Dictionary of British Architects*, New Haven and London 1995 (3rd edition)

G.E.C. (ed. V. Gibbs) *The Complete Peerage of England, Scotland and Ireland*, London 1910–1959

Burke's Peerage

The Scots Peerage, Edinburgh 1904–1914

Picture Acknowledgements

The publishers wish to thank the following for permission to reproduce pictures.

The Collection of K. Adam: 62.

The Trustees, British Museum, copyright © British Museum: 49 (top).

Hodder and Stoughton Ltd, photograph by Brian Long first published in Nigel Tranter, *The Queen's Scotland: The North East* (London,1974): 33 (top) .

Museum of Antiquities, Edinburgh: 14.

National Library of Scotland: 15.

National Library of Scotland (Map Library): 38–39, 40, 56–57.

National Galleries of Scotland: 36, 45.

Rex Features for photographs by Jeremy Sutton Hibbert: 18 (top), 19.

Royal Commission for the Ancient and Historical Monuments of Scotland: Crown Copyright 4–5, 34–35, 96, 97, 112 (bottom), 142–143, 152, 154.

Scottish Highland Photo Library, Tain: 16, 37 (top).

Scottish National Portrait Gallery: 65, 115.

Scottish Record Office: 60–61, 143.

Tain & District Museum: 17, 20–21, 26, 43 (top), 52, 59.

A Scottish Private Collection: 25.

Other illustrations

Fritz von der Schulenburg: 7, 8–9, 10–11,12. 13 (top), 18 (bottom), 22, 23 (top), 41, 43 (bottom), 53 (bottom), 58, 64, 66 (bottom), 67, 68–69, 71 (top), 73, 74 (top), 77, 79, 93, 98–99, 100, 101, 102, 103, 106–107, 108–109, 110 (top), 111, 112, 114–115, 116, 117(top), 118, 120, 121, 122–123, 124, 125, 126–127, 128, 129, 130–131, 132-133, 134, 135, 136, 137, 138-139, 142–143, 144–145, 156.

D.S. Wormell: 28, 47, 49 (bottom), 53 (top), 75, 76–77, 119 (top).

Balnagown Archive: 3, 13 (bottom), 37 (bottom), 55, 74 (bottom), 78, 80, 81, 82, 83, 84, 85, 86, 87, 88, 89, 90, 91, 95, 106–107, 121.

Balnagown Estates (photographs: Scottish National Portrait Gallery Archive): 46, 54, 70.

W. Macgill, *Old Ross-shire and Scotland* (Inverness, 1909): 30, 118 (bottom).
William Taylor, *The History of Tain* (Tain, 1882): 27.
Thomas Bewick, *The History of Quadrupeds*: 66 (top).
C.R.B. Barrett, *The 85th King's Light Infantry* (London, 1913): 71 (bottom).

Index

PREVIOUS PAGES: *The wall paintings in an alcove of the Trophy Room include a dragon and a club wielding Highlander, perhaps representing one of the savages who appear as supporters in the Ross coat of arms.*
RIGHT: *A cigarette-lighter in the form of a figurine of a soldier of the Seaforth Highlanders (Ross-shire Buffs, Duke of Albany's). The last Sir Charles Ross of Balnagown served as an officer in this Scottish regiment.*

Index

Index

Index

Index